D1128117

WINNING PROPOSALS

WINNING PROPOSALS
Writing to get results

Hans Tammemagi, Ph.D.

Self-Counsel Press
(a division of)
International Self-Counsel Press Ltd.
USA   Canada

Printed in Canada.

First edition: 1995; Reprinted: 1995, 1996, 1997
Second edition: 1999; Reprinted: 2000

Canadian Cataloguing in Publication Data

Tammemagi, H.Y.
    Winning proposals

        (Self-counsel business series)
        Includes bibliographical references.
        ISBN 1-55180-254-6

1. Proposal writing in business. 2. Letting of contracts. 3. Persuasion (Rhetoric). I. Title II. Series.
HF5718.5.T35 1999   808'.066658   C99-910793-3

Self-Counsel Press
(a division of)
International Self-Counsel Press Ltd.

1704 N. State Street	1481 Charlotte Road
Bellingham, WA 98225	North Vancouver, BC V7J 1H1
USA	Canada

CONTENTS

ACKNOWLEDGMENTS

When this voyage began, I was not sure where it would lead. However, many storms have been weathered and a port has been reached. This would not have been possible without the steadfast help and support of many people to whom I am indebted.

A rough first draft was significantly improved by the review of Dr. Lloyd Garner, Mary Anne Hansen, and Dr. Andy Panko. Michael Fancy kindly produced a number of graphic figures. Finally, I would like to thank Allyson McPhee for her moral support during this period.

This book is dedicated to my children, Tiina and Marty.

INTRODUCTION

The purpose of this book is twofold. First, it teaches the rudiments of how to prepare a proposal. The components that you need are listed and described.

However, tools and components are just a collection of pieces unless they can be assembled in a meaningful manner. Thus, the second and more important purpose is to explore the exciting realm of persuasion — making the proposal into a winner. To be a successful persuader, you need to know why people agree to things. From there you can develop essential guidelines that will help you persuade people to accept your proposals and ideas.

This book goes beyond what other books offer in proposal writing — it provides not just formulas and recipes, but also the *psychology* that is needed to make your proposal successful.

The foundation of writing winning proposals lies in the psychology of persuasion, something that is rooted in human nature and does not change over time. Thus, I thought it would be a very long time before an updated edition of *Winning Proposals* would be necessary. This second edition has been prepared a scant five years after the first one, not because there has been some unexpected change in human nature, but rather because of the extraordinary revolution in communications brought about by the Internet. The Internet and the World Wide Web have had an impact on many aspects of life, including proposal writing. This second edition directs you to Web sites that will help you to obtain requests for proposals and that can assist you in writing your proposals.

The motivation for this book arose from my long involvement in the consulting business and also through my association with the academic world. The lifeblood of an engineering consulting firm is the proposal. The consulting firm must write and win a reasonable share of proposals, or perish. University researchers are in the same position; they must prepare good grant applications or wither. Consulting firms and universities need to understand how effective proposals are prepared and devote considerable resources to ensuring that their staff can write proposals of very high quality.

Sadly, my experience has shown that this is not the case. Effective proposal writing is an overlooked discipline; it somehow falls between the cracks. All too often individuals are left to fend for themselves with little or no guidance. In those cases where instruction is provided, the emphasis is generally on the components that make up a proposal and the mechanics of assembling those components, rather than on strategy and psychology.

This is akin to giving a soldier the tanks, guns, and other equipment needed to fight a battle without teaching the tactics necessary to out-maneuver the opponent. It is a common and glaring oversight. This book outlines the important strategies and methods for turning an ordinary proposal into a *winning* proposal.

Another critically important aspect that is often overlooked is how efficiently proposals are prepared. When proposals require less time and effort to produce, considerable savings are realized. Describing how proposals can be prepared efficiently forms an important part of this book. For organizations that submit many proposals, these savings will have a very tangible and direct impact on the bottom line. Your proposals will be more convincing and less costly to prepare. Your competitors had better beware!

Because this book uses proposals to illustrate the art of persuasion, it will be of particular interest to:

- Consulting companies competing for contracts
- University researchers competing for research grants
- Business people who are seeking venture capital

However, as it contains a much broader analysis of the art of persuasion, it will also be of benefit to:

- Salespeople selling the myriad of things they sell
- Fundraisers

In particular, this book is intended for those many people who have bright, innovative ideas and want to bring them to reality.

1
THE FASCINATION OF PROPOSALS

a. The importance of proposals

Throughout my working life, I have been fascinated by proposals. A prime reason for my fascination is the overall importance of the proposal. As our society changes and heavy industry and resource production decreases and the service sector grows in importance, so grows the significance of the proposal. Virtually all parts of the service sector use the formal, competitive proposal to solicit and offer work. Proposals have become one of the most important tools of modern technological business. A proposal is both a sales presentation and a marketing tool. Without the ability to write good, winning proposals, many companies would cease to operate.

Millions of proposals are requested and submitted each year in North America and cover diverse services such as installation of pollution control devices, safety and management training courses, landscaping and interior decoration, surveys of consumer product usage, reviews of cultural behavior, building of bridges and other infrastructure, filling of potholes, and so on. All levels of government as well as most parts of the private sector rely on the competitive proposal as their principal means of awarding contracts. Several billion dollars of goods and services are procured annually using proposals.

In this growing information age, consulting firms are proliferating, and their very existence — be they engineering, environmental, or business management firms — depends on proposals. Any single company might write from a few dozen to several hundred proposals each year. Thus, the lifeblood of a consulting firm is the proposal.

But the importance of the proposal does not end with the consulting firm. In today's business world virtually all firms that offer a service or product must submit descriptions to their clients of what they have to offer and why that service or product is necessary. They must present persuasive proposals. At universities, professors must submit proposals to obtain research grants. Hospitals must present proposals to government to receive operating funds or capital for a new wing or a magnetic resonance imagery unit. Proposals are a vital part of our modern society.

b. Jekyll and Hyde personality

Proposals have a dual personality.

Another fascinating aspect of proposals is their Jekyll and Hyde personality. On the one hand they can be frustrating and difficult. Many people do not enjoy the stress involved in meeting deadlines and having to produce a winner. On the other hand, proposals are fascinating, alluring, and full of reward and satisfaction.

Why do proposals have this complex dual personality? Let's look at the difficulties first. Not many people know how to write a winning proposal. Most firms and educational institutions do not place great emphasis on teaching this subject. Why is this? A proposal is difficult to write; it combines a factual presentation with the psychology of persuasion. In other words, the proposal intertwines science and art. At the same time, the proposal must be very attractive with an appealing layout. It is not easy to combine these attributes.

Furthermore, the proposal is a major document, similar in size to a report or small book, which requires considerable effort to compile. It must contain a well thought-out technical work plan, company credentials and experience, a cost estimate, and other relevant information.

In addition, proposals are often written under intense pressure. To meet the required deadlines frequently means working overtime and disrupting family and private life. There may also be a fear of rejection should the proposal lose; this can be exacerbated by senior managers who may place considerable pressure on the proposal team with a win-at-all-costs attitude.

c. The satisfaction of proposals

On the other hand, there is a very tangible excitement associated with the proposal preparation process. And there is enormous satisfaction in preparing a winning proposal! There is nothing as exhilarating as learning that your proposal has won.

One of the fondest memories of my career was winning my first contract at a firm that I had just joined. The firm was in a dilemma: a major request for a proposal had just been received which involved the development of a large software program for marine engineering design. Unfortunately, the person in charge of this area was on holiday and no one else was prepared to take the lead in the proposal preparation. I volunteered, and although I was a junior person, I was given the green light. I set to work with an enthusiasm that only youth and naiveté can generate. I enlisted the help of a very bright engineer who ensured that the proposal was technically strong, and I tried a number of new slants that my new firm didn't usually employ. We worked long hours and assembled a fine looking document. We took care not only with the technical aspects but also with the visual appearance of the proposal. We used graphs and figures, and a cover was specially designed by computer to reflect the theme of the proposal. I was proud of the final product.

As often happens, almost a month passed after the submission and the daily humdrum of consulting life took my mind completely off that proposal. One day, the president of the firm, who up to that time had never acknowledged my existence, walked into my office and began to heartily congratulate me. My proposal had won. I was ecstatic! My colleagues were ecstatic. The proposal resulted in a major contract, which in turn led to further contracts; the financial contribution to my firm was significant. My reputation at the firm soared and I was accepted as part of the established circle. All this because of one proposal!

A good proposal writer is a valuable commodity, a key person in the firm. He or she is the bread winner, the bringer of contracts and work. A good way of enhancing career growth is to learn the basics of writing good proposals. This skill will be a valuable asset on your resume. As well, as you will see, this skill is transportable and will also help you in other areas of your life.

The excitement associated with every proposal is like buying a lottery ticket. Your mind is racing with thoughts of what you will

There is enormous satisfaction in preparing a winning proposal.

do with the winnings. Every proposal submission brings uncertainty, yet there is also the unbridled hope that is an intrinsic component of the human spirit.

d. The challenge of competition

Proposals also bring the challenge of competition. If you are a natural competitor, you will enjoy writing proposals, for they are the quintessential challenge. You are competing against top firms who are also pursuing the same objective. Like an athlete, you must constantly hone your skills in writing and improve the quality of the product. It is also important to learn to live with the disappointment of losing. It is essential to learn from your defeats so your next proposal will be better. Give everything you have, push to the limit, and make sure you submit the best proposal that can be produced under the given circumstances.

The proposal process is intrinsically competitive.

e. Persuasion

How do you overcome uncertainty? How do you create a winning proposal? *The key is persuasion.* Persuasion can be defined as the process by which a person's attitudes or behavior are, without duress, influenced by communication from other people. In chapter 3, the principles underlying persuasion are discussed. These principles can be applied to make your proposal more persuasive than your competitor's.

Persuasion is powerful and mysterious. It requires a knowledge of the human thinking process, a compassionate understanding of your fellow human beings. What motivates people? How do you look inside another person's mind and quietly bring his or her train of thought onto your track?

Life is a never-ending proposal.

Persuasion is found in all things we do or say, in all parts of our lives. Life is a contest of wits. In this increasingly competitive world, you must sell your ideas, your concepts, and your dreams better than the next person. Whether you are selling cars, houses, major commodities, running for elected office, courting someone romantically, vying for a contract, or convincing senior management to accept your ideas, the gentle art of persuasion is essential to success. As Robert Louis Stevenson stated, "Everyone lives by selling something."

f. Persuasion in business

Although persuasion plays a role in virtually every facet of life, it is an essential part of business. A successful businessperson is always very good at writing winning proposals and applying the gentle art of persuasion in all aspects of his or her business dealings.

The success of the entrepreneur is largely due to an inspired idea. We usually recognize that hard work is also a contributing ingredient in an entrepreneur's success. However, the most important quality — persuasive skill — seldom receives its proper recognition.

Selling the idea, not having the idea, is the real challenge. Persuasion plays a key role from the inception of the entrepreneurial idea through to the mature business operation. First, financial support must be raised by a special type of proposal: a business plan. It must be very persuasive indeed, for there are not many people, even rich ones, who will easily part with their money. Words must be crafted together to form a powerful, persuasive lever with which the mind-set of the venture capitalist or banker must be changed from a dubious to a receptive state and money gently pried from his or her grasp.

Having obtained capital, the entrepreneur must next convince the public to purchase the product or service. Again the entrepreneur is faced with a daunting market challenge, for today's consumer is more sophisticated and is faced with an almost limitless variety of products or services competing for his or her hard-earned savings.

Having passed these two difficult "selling" hurdles, persuasion continues to be a major component of the successful operation of this new enterprise. Now the entrepreneur must persuade the labor force to work at high efficiency and productivity and at the same time to accept labor rates low enough to achieve an economic operation.

The gentle art of persuasion must also be practiced at the decision-making and boardroom level. A successful business operation is seldom run by one person. At some point, partners or principals will be acquired and become involved with key decision making. When human beings interact there is seldom unanimity and so the persuasive skills of the entrepreneur will be continually tested to keep the partners aligned with the vision of the company.

An entrepreneur's greatest asset is not the widget that has been invented, but rather the ability to sell the widget to the world.

Persuasion is an essential part of business.

2
TO BID OR NOT TO BID, THAT IS THE QUESTION

You are ready to embark on the exciting voyage of writing a proposal. Before you set sail on those choppy waters, you need to have a reason for launching the endeavor. Perhaps you are a university researcher and the annual grant application time has arrived. Or you are a fledgling entrepreneur and you have developed an idea and would like to raise some capital to bring it to market. Or you work with a consulting firm and you have received a request for proposal (usually referred to by its abbreviation: RFP).

The request for proposal is a widely used tool for soliciting bids. But how do you proceed when an RFP arrives at your doorstep? You must not respond in a Pavlovian manner and automatically begin preparing a proposal. Many RFPs are unsuited to your firm and you will be wasting your time and money by responding to them. In other instances, even if the work they are soliciting is well within the technical capabilities of your firm, there may be other good reasons for not bidding. In other words, you should not respond to every RFP; you must take the time to make sound, bid-or-not-to-bid decisions.

a. How to get requests for proposals

Before we study how to respond to RFPs, let us look at how to get on the mailing list to receive RFPs in the first place.

Writing the proposal is only one step, albeit an important one, in an overall process that begins long before the RFP arrives at your doorstep. The proposal process actually starts when you first make the decision to enter a specific market. You must study the market,

The main purpose of an RFP is to elicit competition.

define your potential clients, and persuade them that your firm or organization can provide the services they need. Once you convince them, they will seek your expertise by sending you RFPs.

Private companies generally issue requests for proposals by mailing them directly to companies that they feel have relevant expertise. However, they will often supplement this process by placing ads in newspapers and trade magazines. Frequently, they will also announce RFPs on their Web sites. You should ensure that your firm is on the mailing lists, and that you regularly review relevant newspapers, magazines, and Web sites.

The largest issuer of RFPs is the government. In the United States, the federal government issues contracts with a value of approximately $170 billion each year! Due to its sheer size, the procurement process can be complex. However, a little bit of research, particularly using the World Wide Web, can guide you through this maze.

The main source of information regarding government procurements in the United States is the Commerce Business Daily (CBD). Issued five times a week by the Department of Commerce, it lists all government RFPs over $25,000, as well as providing information on contract awards, subcontracting leads, sales of surplus equipment, and foreign business opportunities. It can be viewed at Department of Commerce and Small Business Administration field offices, or you can order a subscription by writing to the Superintendent of Documents, U.S. Government Printing Office, Washington, D.C., 20402. The best way to view the CBD, however, is on-line. The CBD can be accessed at their Web site, www.cbdweb.com. An annual subscription fee will allow you to perform unlimited keyword searches; you can also define keyword profiles that will be searched whenever you want.

The U.S. Small Business Administration has a useful Web site at sbaonline.sba.gov/expanding that (under the heading, "Procurement") provides guidance to help small businesses sell to the government, including advice on how to write proposals.

Another useful source of information, which will help you identify the government agencies that need your services, is the *U.S. Government Purchasing and Sales Directory,* which can be ordered from the U.S. Government Printing Office, Washington, D.C., 20402. Specify stock number 378-8310-82-13.

In Canada, an electronic tendering service called MERX has been developed that is the official provider of all federal procurement. It also is the official provider for seven provinces and hundreds of hospitals, universities, and school boards. (Links are provided to the Web sites of the three provinces who are not listed in MERX). All RFPs that exceed $25,000 go through MERX.

Searches for relevant RFPs can be done on the MERX Web site at no charge. Alternately, for a fee, they can do daily searches on your behalf and notify you whenever an appropriate RFP is issued. Bid documents can be obtained, for a charge, by downloading via Internet, FAX, mail, or courier. To learn about the MERX system and how it works, log into their Web site at .merx.cebra.com.

Before exploring the complexities of the to-bid-or-not-to-bid question, let's look at the RFP itself.

b. The request for proposal (RFP)

What is the objective of an RFP? The issuer of the RFP has a problem that requires a solution. Instead of requesting a single vendor to provide the service, a number of them are being asked to submit proposals. Thus, the main objective of the RFP is to elicit competition. The purpose of the competitive process, in turn, can be to obtain the lowest price, the best quality, an innovative approach, or some combination of the above. (Of course, occasionally the winner has already been selected and the RFP is only being issued because the organization's policy is to obtain at least three quotes.)

Information that must be provided to the competitors includes *what* is to be provided, *why* it is needed, and *when* it must be provided. In addition, the RFP lays out the terms and conditions for performing the work. The RFP may vary from a few pages to many pages for larger contracts. In particular, government RFPs tend to be larger and more complex. As a general rule, the size and complexity of the RFP is directly related to the size of the bureaucracy of the issuing organization.

Remember, the client has a problem. Furthermore, the client is convinced that the problem can and should be solved and has expended time and resources to prepare and issue the RFP. In most cases the client has also set aside the budget for the project.

RFPs do not have a set format and their style and length can cover a wide spectrum. Nevertheless, certain features are generally a standard part of the RFP. These include the following elements.

1. Title page

The title page includes the project title, issuer of the RFP, reference or file number, and date of issue.

2. Introduction and background

The introduction and background which includes the need for the work and any relevant information such as the earlier phases of the work.

3. Scope of the work

The scope of the work, which is the most important part of the RFP, outlines the work the consultant must perform. It is usually divided into a number of tasks. It is important that you understand *exactly* what service or product is to be provided. The scope is not always intended as a definitive statement of work, but rather may be an indication of some of the approaches to the problem. You should clarify before starting whether you are limited to the suggested scope or can submit different ones for equal or even preferred consideration.

You must also recognize that the RFP may be less than perfect. For example, the writer of the RFP is often not an expert in this field. He or she may have prepared the RFP in a rush or simply may not have very good writing skills. Communicate with the client's representative to ensure that you fully comprehend the scope of work.

4. Schedule

The schedule describes the timetable to which the work is to be performed. It usually specifies the total period of time over which the work must be performed, such as six months. It often also specifies intermediate milestones.

5. Project budget

Occasionally the client will specify the value of the contract. Usually, however, this item of information is carefully guarded and is not divulged in the hope that this will result in lower bids. If it is not specified, you should strive to obtain at least a ballpark budget target. This is vitally important information, particularly when open-ended projects are involved, and will help you enormously with the difficult decision of how to price your proposal.

Once we received an RFP for a site assessment of health and environmental impacts of a 25-year-old abandoned landfill. We were quite concerned because the project was very open-ended, yet no budget was specified by the government agency issuing the RFP. We decided to call the agency and inquire.

As usually happens, the person in charge stated that this information could not be released. When I persisted, stating that the scope of work was very general and we needed some guidance, she said that she would check with her boss and get back to me. Much to my surprise, she called back the following day and gave a budget range of $45,000 to $50,000, which was considerably lower than we had estimated. I don't believe this information was supplied to any of the other bidders. The story had a happy ending as, armed with this information, we won the bid.

Always inquire about the budget when it is not specified. You may not always receive as positive a response as in this story, but you will usually get some clues.

6. Cost of the work

The RFP will request that you provide a price or quotation for the service or product you are providing. It will also outline the level of detail you must provide for your quotation. In general, you should expect to provide a cost breakdown by task including further breakdown by labor, equipment, materials/supplies, subcontracts, travel/living, and taxes. You may also, usually for government departments, be requested to indicate your profit separately.

7. Payment method

The RFP will also generally stipulate the method by which the client will pay you. For example, payment alternatives include a lump sum at the successful conclusion of the contract (this is best suited to contracts of short duration), monthly payments for labor and expenses incurred in the preceding month, or lump sum payments when pre-established milestones are reached during the course of the contract. Other payment methods are also possible, but whatever they are, they should be described in the RFP.

8. Evaluation criteria and contractor selection

The issuer usually has a method of evaluating the proposals that are received, ranking them, and selecting the best one. It is common to use a formal evaluation process in which each proposal is reviewed and marked against certain criteria. Appropriate criteria are selected that reflect those aspects that are important to the issuer. For example, price may be of less importance than technical quality and this would be reflected by having a higher score for technical approach.

Typical criteria for a complex technical consulting project might be:

- **Technical proposal**

Understanding of scope, objectives	10
Proposed technical approach	30
Recognition of potential problems	20

- **Corporate and staff qualifications**

Key personnel	10
Team organization	5
Previous experience	9

- **Management proposal**

Work plan and schedule	5
Project manager qualifications	5
Management capability	6
TOTAL	100

In this example the client wants to be assured that not only the technical approach to the problem is sound, but that the firm also has the staff and experience to perform the project successfully.

Price can be included in the contractor selection process in a number of ways. One way is to add an additional criterion for price. That is, the lowest price would score a certain number of points, say 50. In this case the total achievable score would be 150. Alternatively, all companies who score below a certain total score, say 75, would be deemed non-compliant. Of the remaining firms, the one offering the lowest price would be the winner. Other variations are possible.

Whether the issuer of the RFP is doing a formal or informal evaluation, it is important that you understand the criteria that will be used so that you can provide the necessary information in your proposal.

9. Pre-bid meeting

For larger bids, the client may call a pre-bid meeting where the consultants can ask questions and view relevant documents and facilities.

Make sound go or no-go decisions; they are crucial.

10. Post-bid interview

Occasionally, after the proposals have been evaluated, a short list of about three to six firms is selected and may be interviewed to choose the final winner. The requirement, times, and locations for these meetings should be specified in the RFP. The post-bid interview is very important and will be discussed in further detail in chapter 8.

11. Contractual details

The RFP may include a copy of the contract that must be entered into by the winning firm. In this case, you should very carefully review the contract, especially those clauses dealing with liability.

12. Administrative details

There are many administrative details included in the RFP including the following:

(a) The date the proposal is due. Usually this is iron-clad. You must meet the deadline, and if you are even a few minutes late, the bid will be returned unopened.

(b) The number of copies of the proposal to be submitted, usually about three to five. (Occasionally there are requests for an inordinately large number of copies. My firm was once involved in a bid for a state agency that requested 35 copies of the proposal! Unfortunately, we meekly complied with this specification, at a rather high expense, considering that we lost the bid. In retrospect, this was a mistake. If confronted with this kind of request, you should discuss it with some of the other bidders, if you know who they are, and collectively lodge a formal complaint. Alternately, you could simply submit, say, six copies of the proposal stating why you are doing so. I believe that the RFP issuer is being unrealistic and unethical in asking the bidders to cover costs the issuer should bear.)

(c) The address where the proposals are to be delivered.

(d) The contact person acting on behalf of the issuer and his or her telephone and fax number.

(e) The format for the proposal. This section will specify how the issuer wants the qualifications, technical section, costs, etc. presented. Occasionally, a page limit is specified. For example, the proposal may be limited to ten pages or less.

(f) Certifications. The issuer may request that the consultant have an authorized representative of the firm sign the proposal, that is, someone who has the power to bind the company. In addition, the RFP may require certifications regarding conflict of interest, or Canadian or American content, etc. It is important that you read the RFP carefully and identify all certifications that you must supply.

c. It's a statistical game

Writing proposals is a game of probabilities. Just like a gambler at a race track or at the gaming tables of Las Vegas, you must know your statistics and play the odds intelligently. If you let your emotions take control, or if you don't study the form sheet carefully, you will have a sad day at the track. You can't bet on a hunch or some undefined gut feeling; you must do your homework. It is essential that you have all the information possible so you can swing the odds in your favor.

Proposals and bid-or-not-to-bid decisions are a statistical game.

You cannot bet on every horse in every race. Likewise, it is a serious mistake to chase every RFP that comes in. The laws of statistics will ensure that you do not win every proposal. Even the most persuasive and most elegant proposal writer will not have every proposal accepted.

Thus, one of the most important decisions that you as a proposal writer face is whether or not to respond when an RFP arrives. If you work for a consulting firm, your ability to consistently make sound bid-or-not-to-bid decisions will have a major impact on the overall profitability of your firm. One of the most effective ways of increasing your odds is to submit proposals only when you have a reasonably good chance of winning. Specifically, you should drop some of the bids that will likely lose, while retaining the ones that have a good chance of winning.

You cannot afford to waste hard-earned revenue pursuing RFPs which you have little or no chance of winning. The number of respondents to an RFP can vary from as low as 3 to more than 20. Only one of these proposals will be the winner. A reasonable success rate for an established consulting firm is about 20% to 35%.

It is astonishing how ad hoc the bid-or-not-to-bid decision is at many organizations. Under the pressure of a looming submission deadline, and perhaps the need to bring in more revenue, the decision is often made in a non-quantitative manner, generally using the experience of one or two key decision makers, and often using more wishful thinking than science. This chapter helps you make this important decision as objectively and quantitatively as is possible. After all, a great deal of money is riding on this decision and the more objective you are the better the decision will be.

The bid-or-not-to-bid decision contains many imponderable issues and it is impossible to make your RFP 100% on target even a fraction of time. Some maverick manager may decide to respond to an RFP even when all the signals and logical analysis indicate that it should not be pursued. And much to everyone's amazement, he or she lands it! At other times, you may feel that the client must have been thinking of your firm and had your corporate material in hand when he or she wrote the RFP and laid out the specifications. You and your colleagues may concur that it would be impossible to lose the bid. To your utter devastation, when the results are announced, you have lost to some up-and-coming firm that proposed a very innovative approach and was suitably rewarded.

With practice you will discover that psychic powers are not required to make the correct bid-or-not-to-bid decision. Rather, some good investigative analysis, coupled with a dose of hard-nosed and clinical business decision making, will aid you considerably.

Once, my firm received an RFP and at our bid-or-not-to-bid meeting we reached the unanimous conclusion that we could not win. There were two exceptionally well-qualified firms that had better technical expertise and that had been involved in earlier phases of the work as well. We agreed that even if we grossly underbid the contract, one or the other of the two main competitors would probably do likewise, and we would still not be any closer to winning.

But this time, we submitted a proposal anyway for a totally different reason. A new, very large phase of work was beginning of which this RFP represented the first of a long series. We wanted to attract the attention of the client and send a strong signal that we were committed to being involved in the new phase of their program. We were using the proposal as a marketing tool to position ourselves for future work, rather than with the objective of winning this contract. To our utter amazement, we were awarded the contract.

Many months later we discovered that the bids of both our main rivals were being delivered to the client by the same courier company and were in the latter stages of their journey when the van met with a minor mishap. A parcel containing ink was spilled and defaced the bid packages of our competitors obliterating the address to which they were to be delivered. By the time the mess was resolved, the deadline for the submission had passed and the purchasing department of the client would not accept the bids. We won the contract only because of a most unlikely chain of events.

The moral of the story is that making bid-or-not-to-bid decisions is not a black or white process. It is a statistical game and deviations from the norm can always happen. However, statistical processes also follow rules. In particular, most statistical processes have an average outcome with a standard deviation which describes how far about the average the outcomes will be scattered.

The information in the remainder of this chapter will help you improve the quality of your decision making and raise your average. There will continue to be variations about that average, both good and bad, but generally, you will be making better decisions. And when your bid-or-not-to-bid decision making improves, you will win more contracts and will waste less time on losing proposals. This translates directly into improved profit.

d. A standardized approach

To help raise the quality of the bid-or-not-to-bid decision, I recommend that you adopt a standardized approach. This will provide consistency and help ensure that no important factors are overlooked.

The cornerstone of your standardized system should be a standard bid-or-not-to-bid decision form. It will greatly assist the decision-making process by listing the questions that need to be considered by you and your fellow decision makers. For an example, see Sample #1. When you are ready to use a decision form for a particular proposal, circle the appropriate score for each category. It may be useful to have several people complete a form.

In the scoring system, an A denotes a very good or excellent factor and it highly favors your chances of winning the bid. A B denotes it is adequate and C means it is less than adequate. The letter D is used for a factor that is very unfavorable. If you score even one D you should have serious reservations about proceeding with that proposal. For example, in the first decision factor, technical qualifications, a D would imply that your firm lacks the capability to perform this work.

Let's look now at the 11 decision factors that the form poses.

SAMPLE #1
PROPOSAL DECISION FORM

Client: _____

Project Description: _____

Due Date: _____

		Score		
1. Technical qualifications	A	B	C	D
2. Contract value (our share)	A	B	C	D
3. Potential profitability	A	B	C	D
4. Competition (list them)	A	B	C	D
5. Unique selling points (list them)	A	B	C	D
6. Resources to write proposal	A	B	C	D
7. Proposal preparation cost	A	B	C	D
8. Spin-off or follow-on business	A	B	C	D
9. Enhances strategic plan or prestige	A	B	C	D
10. Liability or risk	A	B	C	D
11. Other factors	A	B	C	D

A = Highly favorable

B = Adequate

C = Less than adequate

D = Very unfavorable (e.g., you do not have the technical capability; you would lose money; the job is "wired" to an opponent)

1. Technical qualifications

Technical qualifications are fundamental! Even with the inspiration gained from this book, you cannot write a winning proposal unless you have the product or the expertise to provide the service the client needs.

It is best if the necessary expertise can be drawn completely from your own company; however, we are living in a complex technological age and you may need specialized subconsultants. There is nothing wrong with supplementing your team with outside expertise. In fact, using subconsultants may enhance the image of the team and increase the probability of winning. It is important that you have in place a network of specialty subconsultants to draw from.

However, there is a fine line to walk. You must be perceived by the client as providing the largest and most important part of the work. The client does not want to pay you to oversee the work of others; in most cases the client could do this himself or herself.

Don't oversell your qualifications. This strategy will soon catch up with you and your credibility will be lost. You should objectively evaluate the strength of your technical qualifications as being excellent, good, adequate, or inadequate.

Include relevant experience as part of this factor (or add it as a separate consideration). Even with good technical expertise, if you have not performed specifically this kind of project, you are unlikely to beat out an experienced firm. It is not enough that you *can* do the job, you must be *seen* to be able to do it.

If there is more than one key technical area, you may wish to repeat this category of your proposal decision form for each area.

2. Your contract value

You must have a good estimate of the contract value. Often this is specified in the RFP. If it is not, you *must* contact the client and request this information. Quite often they are reluctant to provide a budget figure, but you should persist. They will almost always give some idea of the approximate budget they have earmarked for the project or at the very least they will provide some clues to whether it is a high or low priority issue to them. Clearly, the higher the priority, the more likely they have assigned a realistic budget. And you should be able to estimate that budget with some confidence; after all, you are an expert in this field, or you wouldn't have received an RFP.

For this line of the proposal decision form, contract value refers only to the value which accrues to your firm. For a complex proposal there may be a number of subconsultants or other disbursements that do not bring revenue to your firm; they are just passed through. These should be subtracted from the anticipated contract value. You should then rate your contract value as being large, medium, or small. This assessment of contract size will depend on the size of your organization and the nature of your business. What may seem a very big contract to a smaller firm may be trivial to a large corporation.

3. Potential profitability

Potential profitability takes into consideration the nature of the client, the pricing strategy of your competitors, and other factors. The situation is excellent if it is a large contract and the client is seeking a quality product and is willing to pay a fair price to obtain it. In this case you would be able to bid with a good markup (this would merit a ranking of A). On the other hand, the client may be a notorious scrooge and, in addition, there may be some very hungry competitors. In this instance you may feel that you can only win the contract by bidding at a loss (this would merit a C or D).

Another consideration is that profit is usually better if the contract is for work with which you are very familiar. In contrast, work that is out of your main area of expertise will require some learning on the job and more time, most of which will not be billable. In this case the overall bottom-line profit will be lower. Your ranking should reflect such circumstances; your tendency to bid should become lower as your potential profitability becomes lower.

4. How do you rate against the competition?

Make a list of the probable competitors. Usually, the greater the number of bidders, the smaller your chances of winning. An important consideration is whether another firm has done the earlier phases of the project. Or does one of the competitors have the world's most eminent authority on their team?

It is unfortunate, but occasionally there are instances where the winning bidder has already been selected, but due to the issuing agency's regulations they are required to obtain at least three competitive bids. You should do your best to ferret out these situations. You must be realistic and assign a C or D if you feel the contract is "wired" to someone else, or if there are some very well-placed competitors.

Be realistic; avoid the common pitfall of wishful thinking.

5. Unique selling points (USPs)

Do you have some good unique selling points (USPs) that make you stand out from the crowd? Some USPs might be:

- You can offer the best price
- You have an acknowledged national expert on the team
- You performed the earlier phase of the work
- Your firm is located near the project area
- A former senior manager of the client now works for your firm
- You have an appropriate network of offices for this project

USPs are one of the most important persuaders in a proposal, and without them your proposal will suffer. They are discussed further in chapter 4.

6. Resources to write the proposal

Preparing a proposal is hard work, and good proposals take time to prepare. Make sure the resources are available to obtain a quality product without a panic-stricken rush at the last minute. Is your best proposal writer available or is he or she on holidays? Is secretarial support available or is everyone committed to an important report? Make sure that there is sufficient time available to prepare the proposal. Time is a particularly valuable resource.

7. Proposal preparation cost

The cost of preparing proposals can vary widely. Some clients will issue a major RFP and only request a brief letter proposal. Other (usually government) organizations request a much more elaborate presentation and can also require that it be preceded by a statement of qualifications (SOQ), which is a two-phase proposal that is considerably more expensive to prepare. In addition, the client sometimes stipulates a mandatory pre-bid meeting. If this is located at some distance from your office it could be very expensive to attend.

We once sent two of our staff over 3,000 miles to attend a mandatory pre-bid meeting on the opposite coast. It was a major contract that we unfortunately lost. We could have prepared two or three proposals just for the cost of the trip alone.

In addition to pre-bid meetings, the client might also conduct interviews of the firms that make the short list after the bid has been submitted. In the worst case, you might be required to submit first an SOQ and then a proposal, as well as attend a pre-bid meeting and also an interview. You might invest all this effort and then lose the bid. If you are going to suffer the indignation of this nightmare, there should be some very tangible compensating features to the contract. Do not bid on a contract requiring such elaborate effort unless it is a multi-million dollar job or you have some other very compelling reason to bid. For anything less, the client has lost touch with reality and is making unreasonable demands.

8. Spin-off or follow-on business

Often an RFP represents the first phase of a much larger project. You must consider if there are subsequent phases that you would obtain on a sole-source basis, or if this contract would give you a considerable advantage for bidding. What is the size of any such potential follow-on work? Clearly, a once-off project is less enticing than one that leads to substantial additional work.

9. Enhances strategic plan

You should determine if this project fits into the strategic plan for your firm or if it is a peripheral exercise. For example, it may be a project that is part of the mainstream of your firm and it would be a loss of face not to submit a bid. Or perhaps, it represents a new area that your management has targeted for penetration. Occasionally there is a project that would significantly enhance the reputation and image of your firm.

A standardized approach will save you time.

10. Liability or risk

You should assess the potential liability associated with the project. For example, larger engineering projects, or ones that involve contaminants, may have significant potential for liability. Liability could arise by your inability to fulfill the scope of work within the budget or schedule or by delivering a faulty or incorrect final product (this can include reports).

There may be costs involved through potential lawsuits, by having to purchase professional errors and omissions insurance (which is generally quite expensive), or simply by having to redo major parts of the project at your own cost.

Your ranking of this category on your proposal decision form should reflect the potential liability of the project and the associated costs.

11. Other factors

In addition, you need to determine and quantify if there are benefits in addition to those considered above. For example, if your office is not very busy you may, out of desperation, pursue some less probable RFPs.

Once the form is completed, you will need to review it and make a bid-or-not-to-bid decision. If you have circled a single factor in column D (the reject column) you should not proceed unless there are some very compelling circumstances. To proceed, most of your circled items should be in columns A or B.

e. Using the proposal decision form for follow up

The form presented in Sample #1 not only will assist you in making sound decisions but will provide a useful way to document your decision-making process. You should file the completed forms along with a record of the decision that was reached. Periodically, you can review them, taking into consideration the results of those RFPs for which you submitted proposals. Over time you will develop a statistical database that will allow you to quantify, to some degree, the quality of your decision making. In addition, you will be able to assess whether your statistical average for winning proposals is rising. The feedback provided by such periodic analysis will give you confidence and will help you in your efforts to continually improve your proposals.

If your firm is large with many divisions and many offices located across the country, the bid-or-not-to-bid decision is likely made in different ways in each office. The proposal decision form can be a useful tool to provide consistency in approach across the company.

If your organization submits a large number of proposals and wishes to be more rigorous (i.e., quantitative) in its approach, you can assign a numerical score for each line instead of the letters. The maximum possible score for each factor would be set, or weighted, to reflect its importance. For example, "technical qualifications" might be assigned a higher maximum score (like 10, 5, and 1 for A, B, C, respectively) than "resources to write proposal" (using 5, 3, and 1 for A, B, C, respectively). A total score would be calculated for each proposal and you would need to exceed a certain pre-established score to proceed. The pre-established scores would be developed over time as your firm gained experience and sufficient data was accumulated to form statistically significant guidelines.

Sample #2 shows a decision form completed for an RFP that my firm received. The RFP was for an investigation of an old railway and industrial site that was contaminated with a variety of pollutants. Developing and costing a remedial action plan was an important part of the contract. As is shown, we felt that technical qualifications, unique selling points, and spin-off business were the most important factors for this bid, and we assigned maximum scores of 20, 20, and 15, respectively, for them.

As shown, our total score was 86 out of 105, or 82%. This is a high score and shows that we were well qualified to perform the work and could assemble a strong bid with unique features that would make us stand out from the rest of the competitors. In this case we had worked for this client before and were familiar with the site in question. The decision to proceed with a proposal was reached quickly.

As experience is gained, the scores and guidelines can be refined and your confidence in, and quality of, the decision-making process will increase.

If quantitative scoring is used as part of the decision form, then it would be well suited for setting up on a personal computer using spreadsheet or similar software. If the computers in your firm are linked by a network and you use electronic mail, you could make the bid-or-not-to-bid decision very quickly without ever meeting face-to-face with your colleagues.

I must emphasize that the decision form is only a tool. It cannot replace human judgment. Making the decision to bid or not to bid is very complicated and you can never be assured of being 100% correct. There will always be information that is missing and there will always be a place for intuition and gut feeling. Making the bid-or-not-to-bid decision is an art, not a science and always will be. However, the decision form will act as a checklist and it will help ensure that you are being objective, not emotional.

The decision form is most useful when you have a difficult decision, that is, in borderline cases and in those cases when you should not bid. Usually it is easy to identify RFPs that you are qualified for. It is psychologically much more difficult to say no, and the decision form will help you make that tough decision.

By providing a framework for the decision-making process, the decision form should help in reducing a great source of frustration for the proposal writing team. All too often the bid-or-not-to-bid decision is a vexing, time-consuming process that wends its way

SAMPLE #2
COMPLETED PROPOSAL DECISION FORM
(Using a numeric scoring system)

Client: <u>Federal Environmental Group</u>

Project Description: <u>Industrial Site Investigation and Cleanup</u>

Due Date: <u>November 13, 200-</u>

	Maximum Score	**Our Score**
1. Technical qualifications	20	17
2. Contract value (our share)	10	7
3. Potential profitability	5	5
4. Competition (list them)	5	3
5. Unique selling points (list them)	20	16
6. Resources to write proposal	5	5
7. Proposal preparation cost	5	4
8. Spin-off or follow-on business	15	15
9. Enhances strategic plan or prestige	10	8
10. Liability or risk	5	2
11. Other factors	5	4
TOTAL	105	86 (82%)

Note: Generally a score of greater than 70% is necessary to proceed.

through various levels of management, greatly reducing the limited time available for preparing the proposal. By establishing a routine and standardized process, the time required for reaching the decision should be reduced substantially.

3

WHAT IS PERSUASION?

Edison said genius is 1% inspiration and 99% perspiration. The same is true for successful proposals. They require a lot of work and perspiration. However, the key is the remaining 1% of inspiration, or in the case of proposals, the winning psychology. This chapter focuses on that 1%. It inspects and dissects the topic of persuasion and gives you many ideas on how to give your proposal that winning edge.

Persuasion permeates all facets of human interaction and is an essential component in virtually all of our endeavors. But how are people persuaded to do certain things? What factors influence a person so that one agrees to what another is proposing? What techniques are involved? Can these techniques be applied to proposal writing?

The answer to the last question is an emphatic yes. Psychologists have devoted considerable energy to the study of compliance and have identified the general principles that control persuasion. The importance of persuasion has received recognition throughout the centuries and persuasion has been treated an art, a craft, and a science by the great cultures. Aristotle and Cicero devoted entire treatises to the topic. In European universities in the Middle Ages, persuasion was considered a basic liberal art and was avidly studied by all scholars. In our modern world, persuasion, in the form of advertising, supports a major industry.

The gentle art of persuasion has roots that penetrate deep into the human psyche. An understanding of persuasion requires an understanding of how the human mind works and how our society functions. There are basic human patterns and reflex conditionings that have evolved over the eons and that play an important role in persuasion.

Thus, to understand persuasion, which includes the preparation of winning proposals, you must understand human beings. We need to know ourselves. It is essential to have a knowledge of how we as human beings are motivated. An understanding of and sympathy toward others is an important first step toward successful persuasion.

An excellent example of how these principles are applied is the operation of compliance professionals. These are the persuasion artists who sell vacuum cleaners and encyclopedias, raise funds, design advertising, and many others who very professionally persuade people like you and me to part with our money.

Although we may not always agree with the ethics of some of these compliance professionals, they are very good at what they do. And the reason is that their techniques have evolved and been perfected over a long period of time. These techniques have a solid foundation in the fundamental principles of persuasion and there is much that we can learn from them. Let us have a look at a compliance professional applying the power of persuasion.

a. A compliance professional at work

The best real-life example of the power of persuasion that I have ever witnessed began rather quietly. On returning home from an exhausting day at the office, I was somewhat annoyed to learn that my wife had arranged for a gentleman to demonstrate a vacuum cleaner to us. Penelope had fallen prey to the offer that in return for viewing the demonstration, she was guaranteed to win a prize from a draw. The prizes included a trip to Florida and a new car.

"Calm down dear," she explained. "It will do you no harm to miss half an hour of snoozing on the couch after dinner. Besides, we need a new vacuum cleaner."

"Tonight? But I'm dead tired! And my lumbago is acting up and I have a splitting headache."

My pleas fell on deaf ears. The prize was attainable only if both spouses were present. Well, never mind, thought I, we'll soon send this fellow packing and I will quietly regain the couch.

The doorbell rang at exactly seven that evening. Arousing myself from the couch to open the door, I noticed that the salesman was neatly dressed, and, more surprisingly, he was driving a large, new, and very shiny Lincoln, beside which my humble family vehicle paled. This was my first foreboding that perhaps this chap was very successful at plying his trade.

The salesman proceeded to get the matter of the prize out of the way very quickly. First he stressed that it was not a prize but rather a gift from his company. Then a number was drawn and we became the fortunate recipients of a deluxe carpet cleaning. He waxed eloquent about the extraordinary quality of the cleaning service and how our "gift" was valid for one year.

Next he described the many features of the vacuum cleaner. To my surprise it was constructed of materials that had evolved from the space program. The company behind it was one of the largest and most financially solvent in North America. He showed many glossy pictures of happy users and their endorsements. The coup de grace involved his spilling a bag of dirt on our carpet and then cleaning it very easily and thoroughly with the superb machine.

Unknown to me, the salesman had already accomplished several important objectives. He had established his authority with the Lincoln, he created a feeling of indebtedness with the gift, and he had established the technical superiority of the vacuum cleaner. Next, he moved to close the deal. He first laid the groundwork.

"Surely your dear wife, who toils many hours in this home, deserves a top-of-the-line vacuum cleaner so she can perform her chores more effectively and efficiently?"

I could but lamely agree. He then got Penelope to admit that good quality has no price limit.

Finally, he named the price — a staggering $1,400. As we blanched at this announcement, he quickly noted that surely Penelope deserved the best. As we continued to gasp, he also noted that he could allow a generous trade-in on our existing vacuum. Noting our continuing resistance, he asked what we thought would be a fair price for a machine of such fine quality. Not knowing the price of vacuum cleaners, I guessed that it should be several hundred dollars less than his quoted number. The salesman sadly noted that he agreed and would love to sell it to us for a substantially lower price, but that this would cut his margin to a dangerously low level. He agonized for a while and finally, his voice quivering with emotion, he said that he would telephone his boss and see if a deal could be made at a lower price.

After some time on the telephone, the salesman returned beaming with delight. His boss, recognizing that month end was near, was willing to let this vacuum cleaner go for $1,100, but only with the trade-in included, and only if the deal was concluded tonight. The salesman very confidentially informed us that this was the best deal he had ever been allowed to make, and even showed us a thick sheaf of bills of sale for the same vacuum cleaner that were all for greater sums. My heart pounding, I put my signature on the line.

I am sad and embarrassed to report that Penelope and I were the victims of a very polished compliance professional. Against all my better instincts and penny-pinching background, I was persuaded to pay approximately triple the actual value of the vacuum cleaner. It did not come as a major surprise about a year later when a pulley belt broke, that we could no longer find this "very solvent" company to make claim on the lifetime warranty. Our very persuasive salesman had moved on to another town to ply his trade with a fresh batch of gullible customers.

The performance of the vacuum cleaner salesman has left a permanent scar on my psyche, not to mention my pocket book. To this day I marvel at his persuasive skills. I have spent many, many hours wondering how the same techniques apply to everyday life and how they might be applied to my business of consulting engineering and, in particular, to the writing of proposals. If only my persuasive skills were of the same caliber as the vacuum cleaner salesman's!

It was only much later, once I began to study persuasion, that I learned that the subject has been thoroughly studied by psychologists and, indeed, the techniques used by our vacuum cleaner salesman are understood and have been well documented. I have spent considerable time in getting to understand those principles and, more important, in applying those persuasion principles to proposal writing.

Persuasion is based on a number of basic principles.

I must stress that I do not in any way condone the ethics of the vacuum cleaner salesman. Quite the contrary. As a consultant one must develop long-term clients, which can only be done by delivering quality and standing behind it, not by quietly sneaking out of town after the sale. Nevertheless, the vacuum cleaner salesman story illustrates, very effectively, many of the important persuasion principles.

b. The basic principles of persuasion

Psychology, the scientific study of human behavior, has shown that there are a number of basic principles that control how people influence each other. These principles have evolved over many centuries and are very powerful motivators of human behavior. In fact, the successful and cohesive functioning of our society depends to a large degree on practicing persuasion. Thus, an understanding of persuasion is important not only in preparing influential (and winning) proposals, but also in leading a full and satisfying life.

Although there is a broad spectrum of ways that humans can influence each other, R.B. Cialdini in the book *Influence — How and Why People Agree to Things,* outlined some key persuasion motivators that can be classified into seven general categories as follows.

1. Reciprocity or indebtedness

This principle states that we are indebted to another person who has given us something. We are under obligation to repay or reciprocate for that kindness. This is a very powerful human motivator and is deeply rooted in our society. It is a major factor in making society function harmoniously. Reciprocity is widely used and examples flourish from the trading of political favors by our government leaders to the distribution of free samples by manufacturers.

Our vacuum cleaner salesman very effectively used reciprocity twice. First he insisted that the "prize" of a free deluxe carpet cleaning was a gift from his company. His second use of reciprocity was more subtle. In coming down from the high price to a lower price and in arguing with his boss to accept the lower price, he was doing us a "favor" and building strong feelings of indebtedness.

Reciprocity can be used in many ways in dealing with your client and in preparing a proposal. It is relatively inexpensive to give to clients some small item such as a hat or coffee mug with your company name boldly displayed. You should also seek to perform free services for potential clients, such as advising them on some technical problems. The proposal itself might contain some extras that were not requested, such as color photographs, a specially designed cover, or an approach to the problem that is different, and additional, to that requested.

2. Commitment and consistency

This principle states that once we have made a commitment, a decision, or taken a stand, we will encounter strong internal and external pressures to behave consistently with that commitment. Our society values reliability. Being true to your word is seen as a strength, but being inconsistent is considered a sign of weakness and generally is in bad form.

Furthermore, it is often easier to fall back on automatic, consistent, reflex action rather than thinking through a difficult problem. Or often it is easier to make an automatic consistent response and avoid the unpleasantness that you might have to face if the proper course of action were followed.

For example, there was a case where the senior executive of a firm became personally involved in hiring a certain staff member. It became apparent within a few months that this recruit was not fitting into the company very well. Nevertheless, the senior executive continued, almost blindly, to support the newcomer, to the point where a number of other key staff quit. The senior executive wound up inflicting considerable damage on his organization rather than act in a manner that was inconsistent with his original decision.

Commitment is the key, and our vacuum cleaner salesman very nicely sowed the seeds by getting me to "commit" to such statements as "Yes, my wife certainly deserves the best in carrying out her onerous household chores." This technique of beginning with a small commitment and building it into a much larger (and more expensive) commitment is also known as the foot-in-the-door technique and is widely used by compliance professionals.

Commitment is a powerful tool in the pursuit of contracts and it is essential to find ways in which to get the client to make commitments to you and your firm. One way is to pull out all the stops if an RFP is for the first contract of a series. Like the senior executive, the client will have great difficulty changing consultants for the subsequent contracts. Now is the time to muster all your resources and write a very strong and persuasive proposal.

3. Social copying

This principle states that we often decide how we should behave by copying what other people are doing. We view our behavior in a given situation as "correct" depending on the degree we see other people behaving in a similar manner. Social copying works particularly well when you are uncertain how to behave. It becomes almost automatic to copy what others around you are doing. Bartenders and hat check attendants apply this principle when they "seed" their tip jar with some dollar bills. The advertising industry is always keen to illustrate that their product is the fastest growing or most popular. Interviews or action shots of typical people using and endorsing a product are very common.

Our vacuum cleaner salesman certainly had this principle in mind when he showed the glossy pictures of happy users and their endorsements. Even more effective was the thick sheaf of bills of sales for deals that he had recently made in our community.

The social copying principle can be applied in proposals by quoting references from the same network of business as the client and by describing projects that your firm has performed for similar companies.

4. Authority

From birth we are trained to obey authority. We are faced with a continual stream of authority figures like our parents, our school teachers, street crossing guards, police officers, theater ushers and many, many more. Obedience to authority is a fundamental part of our society and is essential for it to function properly. It is not surprising that the authority principle is one of the most powerful compliance motivators.

Authority can be established in a number of ways. The use of titles is effective: we tend to respect a person who has spent years of hard work to achieve a title. Physical appearance, both in stature and dress, is also an effective means of establishing authority.

Our vacuum cleaner salesman used this powerful motivational principle well. To begin with, he was a tall and heavyset man, over six feet in height. He was well dressed in a navy blue suit, not at all dissimilar from what a business person or lawyer might wear. He used a particularly effective authority technique when I inquired about his very elegant Lincoln car.

"Oh yes, I'm particularly proud of that car. My company awarded it to me," he stated very modestly. "I was the salesman of the month for three consecutive months. The president of our firm said it is only the second time in ten years that this has happened."

It was difficult not to be impressed by these statements. He had certainly established his authority.

In writing proposals it is essential to establish the authority of your firm and the proposed staff, particularly the project manager.

This can be done in a number of ways which include showing the academic credentials of your staff, describing any awards your firm has received, and including photos of laboratories or other impressive facilities.

5. Empathy and trust

This principle states that people prefer to agree to the requests of people they like. In other words, we do not want to hurt others' feelings and jeopardize the relationship by saying or doing something that disagrees with them. Trust plays an important role in helping generate emotions of empathy. If we do not trust people, we will not believe what they say, and we certainly will not accept their ideas.

The vacuum cleaner salesman was very good at creating a warm feeling between us. He was neatly dressed and polite. He complimented Penelope about how attractively the living room was decorated. His sales patter was sprinkled with anecdotes and witticisms. Having established a feeling of ease and empathy, he used it effectively by asking questions that required a direct response. That is, it was very clear to us that he wanted a positive answer and that a negative answer would hurt his feelings. Like lemmings, we had been neatly lured to the cliff's edge by the empathy principle.

Trust is a fundamental and integral part of any proposal. It is important to work at building trust; it is equally important to work at not losing it. Trust and empathy are easiest to build through personal contact. You should seek to meet the client face to face at conferences, meetings, or over lunch. Losing trust is easy to do, usually by overstating your capabilities or by not completing the project on schedule, on budget, or to the high technical quality that is expected.

6. Scarcity

It is a well-known fact that we are more keen to acquire something when it is scarce, particularly when there is competition for it. We'll want it less if the item is readily and abundantly available. The entire capitalistic economic system operates on the law of supply and demand, which is simply a different way of stating the scarcity principle. This technique is used widely by compliance and advertising professionals. We are bombarded by ads for sales that will only last for 24 or 48 hours. Or there are only a limited number of items left and once they're sold, no more will be available.

The vacuum cleaner salesman marshalled the scarcity principle into his clever campaign. The reduced price that his boss allowed was only available for a very limited time; only for that evening, in fact. The item itself was not scarce, but the more attractive price certainly was portrayed that way.

The scarcity principle does not lend itself readily to proposal writing as there are usually many consultants competing for the same contract. Nevertheless, there are occasions when you can muster its power into your attack. These moments usually come when the economy is flourishing and there is a strong demand for the services you offer.

7. Uniqueness

Uniqueness is a persuasion principle that permeates all facets of life. Each human being is distinct and unique from all other humans. We value that uniqueness because it is our personal trademark. At first glance it appears that the social copying and uniqueness principles contradict each other. However, they work in harmony. Social copying sets the broad, overall behavioral patterns that we follow. However, we also like to superimpose on that broad social structure our own unique variations.

An example of how the two principles operate together is the dress code for a formal ball. The social copying principle dictates that all the women will wear long, formal gowns. No woman would dare arrive wearing an outfit that was dramatically different, such as jeans or army boots. However, the uniqueness principle is also a major player, and it would be considered a major embarrassment if two women were to arrive at the grand ball wearing identical dresses.

The uniqueness principle is particularly important if competition is involved. In selling new cars, the sales representatives are very keen to recount any unique features that are available, such as tape and compact disc drives, cellular telephone, superb gas mileage, etc.

Our friend, the vacuum cleaner salesman, had this compliance principle clearly in mind as he established the technical superiority of his vacuum cleaner. It was the very best model available and was unique in that regard. The vacuum was made of space age materials and had numerous features not found on other top-of-the-line models.

For proposals, I consider the uniqueness principle to be the most important of the persuasion principles. Proposals are a competitive

For proposals, the uniqueness principle is the most important.

business. The client will usually be evaluating from 3 to 20 bids. You *must* find some ways of making your proposal stick out from the crowd, to be so unique that the client remembers your bid above the rest.

The ways in which you can make your proposal unique are virtually limitless. It depends largely on your imagination and innovation. We will explore some of these methods in the rest of the book. It should become second nature to start devising unique selling points as soon as you receive an RFP.

In summary, the principles of persuasion are the following:

(a) Reciprocity or indebtedness

(b) Commitment and consistency

(c) Social copying

(d) Authority

(e) Empathy and trust

(f) Scarcity

(g) Uniqueness

4
THE SIX-POINT GUIDELINE FOR WINNING PROPOSALS

The visit of the vacuum cleaner salesman provided a firsthand overview of most of the basic persuasion principles. But how does this psychology of persuasion translate into winning proposals? How do you take general persuasion theory and put it into the practice of writing winning proposals? In this chapter we look at how this is done.

It is not a simple matter to take the basic persuasion principles and transform them into a winning proposal. There are virtually endless ways in which to influence proposal evaluators. Just as there are an infinite variety of human beings, each with their own special personality and characteristics, so each client and each proposal is different and must be assessed on its own merits and within the particular set of circumstances that are involved. Nevertheless, the methods that are used in proposal persuasion are all built on the foundation of the persuasion principles described in the previous chapter.

The majority of the methods used to create winning proposals can be summarized by six basic guidelines:

(a) Establish technical credibility.

(b) Use a client-centered approach.

(c) Get the price right.

(d) Write simply.

(e) Add unique selling points.

(f) Go the extra mile.

In preparing a proposal, you should go through each of these guidelines. These are the spices that must be added to the basic components of a proposal to create that extra zest that will make a winner. Like a good chef, you must decide what spices are required, how much, and where they should be sprinkled to add the piquancy that will tickle the palate of the proposal evaluator.

Each of these six guidelines contain, in varying degrees and amounts, the fundamental persuasion principles discussed in the previous chapter. Let us look at each of these guidelines and see what principles are involved and, more important, how you might employ them in your next proposal.

a. Establish technical credibility

Clearly, you cannot win a bid unless you are qualified to do the work. In fact, you would seldom even receive an RFP unless you have a reasonable amount of technical credibility. Strongly reinforce the impression of technical expertise and firmly establish your technical credentials. This guideline is based on the persuasion principle of establishing authority. You need to figuratively put on a police officer's uniform of technical authority.

In addition to corporate credibility, you need to establish the credentials of each member of your project team. As individuals, they need to have educational and job experience that is relevant to the project. Postgraduate degrees and memberships in appropriate professional societies help establish credibility. If your team members have written or published any books, papers, or articles relevant to the subject, that should be highlighted. This information can be provided in capsule resumes, that is, a paragraph or two summarizing the education, experience, and responsibilities of the designated person.

Corporate strength and experience should also be emphasized. Summarize relevant, similar projects that have been performed by your firm. Do not forget to include references to satisfied clients. Remember, endorsements work in all areas of persuasion.

In particular, you should highlight any awards or recognition that your firm has won for work of a similar nature. You might include a photocopy of the newspaper or journal article which announced the award. This is no time to be modest. You are doing yourself and your firm a disservice if, through some feelings of false modesty, you hide your technical strength.

On the other hand, it is imperative that you do not make inaccurate statements. All your technical credibility will instantly vanish if you are caught falsely embellishing your credentials. You and your firm are not like the vacuum cleaner salesman who regularly relocates to a new region in order to stay one step ahead of displeased customers. On the contrary, your objective is to build long-term relations with your clients. This can only be done on a solid foundation of trust.

Credibility is also reinforced if the client sees that your firm is giving the project high priority and appropriate corporate support. Suppose, for example, that the project entails an environmental investigation. The client will certainly feel more comfortable if the environmental division is a key part of your firm with the environmental division manager at a very senior level. On the other hand, the client will not feel that your firm is taking this sector seriously if the environmental group is hidden away, say, as part of the industrial division. It is helpful if the client sees that your firm is committed to this business sector and has put resources and priority behind it.

b. Use a client-centered approach

One of the most serious and often repeated strategic blunders is writing the proposal from your own viewpoint instead of the client's. You must recognize that you are not selling a commodity or service by itself. Rather, you are selling an improvement to the client's operation. You must put yourself in the client's shoes and inside his or her head.

Why is the work being undertaken? What is its purpose? The proposal must address the client's priorities and objectives, and not get wrapped up in an introspective dissertation of the excellent qualities of your product or service.

This approach is related to the empathy and trust principle of persuasion. One of the best ways of inducing a feeling of empathy between you and another person is to show interest in that person. Think of when you have been at a cocktail party or similar social soirée. Which strangers did you find the most attractive and interesting? They were undoubtedly the ones who showed an interest in you by asking questions about your work, your family, or your hobbies. I can almost guarantee that they were not those individuals who chattered constantly about themselves.

You must present yourself as part of the client's team.

Usually an RFP is issued for a relatively specific project or piece of work. It is essential that you understand the underlying reason why this work is being undertaken and relate your proposal to those objectives — not to your own objectives. You need to understand the client's operation and goals. You need to present yourself as part of the client's team, not as a tool that they are temporarily using. This will help lead to a long-term relationship, not just a once-off contract.

It is not always a simple matter to unearth the client's needs. Often the RFP provides only a fuzzy outline of the background to the requested work, and often none is presented at all. You must do some detective work and shine a beam of light into some of the dark corners of their business. What problems are they facing? Why have those problems arisen? Does your firm have the expertise to find solutions? Do they have the resources, time, and management capability to implement the solutions that you might propose? It may require some considerable effort to obtain this information; however, the rewards are bountiful.

Once you have an understanding of the complexities of your potential client's business, you must present solutions for improving that operation. In other words, you are not only providing the specific service or product that has been requested in the RFP, you must place it in the larger context and describe how it improves their business. For example, you should show how it improves one or more of the following:

- Compliance with regulations
- Profits
- Decision-making capability
- Public image
- Competitive edge
- Quality, reliability
- Operating efficiency
- Employee morale
- Employee safety
- Management and organizational structure

You might also show how your proposal eliminates or reduces:

- Inefficiencies and waste
- Conflict
- Adverse criticism

> A knowledge of the client's business is essential; intelligence gathering is a must.

A knowledge of the client's key staff will provide you with direction on how to make your presentation. Almost without exception there are one or two key people, including the project manager, who will make the decisions, be in charge of the RFP, and manage the contract once a consultant is selected. An important part of your investigation is to find out who they are and what kind of people they are. You need to know their positions in the company, their educational backgrounds, their ambitions and aspirations, and if they prefer to deal in details or generalities.

Achieving this client-oriented approach requires an investment in time and effort. If this is a previous or existing client, you will already know quite a lot about his or her business. Do whatever needs to be done to find out the details that you need. Don't guess. Call or visit and talk, talk, talk to the project manager. This can be done without being offensive, although tact is certainly required. Remember, most people like talking about themselves. For example, you should ask questions such as: "Is the schedule of critical concern?" If yes, then your proposal should emphasize your firm's capability to produce results on time. Other important questions include: "Is quality the key? Is price the governing factor? Why are you doing this? Will there be follow up work? Does your senior management support this initiative?"

A number of years ago my firm received an RFP to perform a waste minimization audit at the local factory of a major international firm. This case history, better than any other, illustrates the importance of a client-centered approach.

The firm was a very attractive potential client and we had submitted proposals to them several times in the past, but always without luck. This time, because we were particularly well qualified in this area and because we really wanted this client, we threw budgetary caution to the wind and decided to submit a really top-notch bid that would blow the competition out of the water. We visited the plant and familiarized ourselves with the layout and the industrial processes that were involved. We developed a very thorough plan for how a waste minimization program would be designed and implemented. Nothing was overlooked. In fact, we did much more than prepare a proposal, we actually committed the ultimate consultant's sin and performed some of the work that was to be done under the contract. We developed a superb plan and, as a clincher, we also offered a substantial discount on our labor rates. How could this proposal possibly lose?

Well, the sad outcome of this story is that the unthinkable happened and we lost the bid. We had been so wrapped up in telling the client what we thought was needed that we forgot to find out what the client actually wanted. In this case, the local plant was responding to a directive from international headquarters that all regional plants should implement waste minimization programs under their own budgets. This directive was greeted unenthusiastically because there was a major recession on and the local plant had also recently been directed to institute some dramatic cost-cutting measures.

The contract was awarded to a firm that submitted a one-page proposal with a price approximately 20% lower than ours. We found it particularly vexing that such a short proposal, prepared in perhaps one hour, had beaten our 35-page masterpiece, which had consumed over 140 hours of hard work. It was clear, with hindsight, that the client's objective was to implement the bare minimum necessary to satisfy head office at minimal cost. In this case, the quality of the work was largely irrelevant.

The concept of a client-centered approach has been championed in other forms of selling. For example, the idea of consultative selling advocates that the traditional approach of a salesperson as simply a vendor who sells a product should be replaced. Instead, the salesperson needs to a be a partner with the customer and market the improvement that his or her product can achieve. The concept of a client-oriented approach in your proposal is an application of the same philosophy.

A client-centered approach is mandatory.

c. Get the price right

Price is often the single most important factor in making a winning proposal. It is also one of the most difficult and frustrating aspects of proposal preparation. If you err on the high side you may price yourself out of the market; if you err on the low side you may win the contract but wind up taking a loss on the job. There is no greater disappointment in the consulting business than receiving the top technical mark on a proposal for an important contract, yet losing the bid to another firm that has offered a marginally lower price.

How can you tell whether your proposed price is correct? Is an adjustment necessary? How much should the adjustment be? It's like a reverse auction, except you cannot see the other bids. This section discusses the strategies that you can adopt to make this difficult decision easier, and also more successful.

You need five key pieces of information to be able to build a sound pricing strategy for your proposal. You need to determine —

(a) the "fair" price for the project,

(b) the approximate budget that the client has for this project,

(c) the importance of the price (relative to quality) to the client,

(d) who the competition is and how they will price their proposals, and

(e) the importance of this job to your firm.

1. Fair price

The fair price is a reference or yardstick and is an essential initial step toward developing your final price. The fair price is the price that should be charged for the service or product under fair market conditions. That is, it is the price that would be charged by a typical, qualified firm for delivering a good quality product using normally accepted labor rates and markups and making a reasonable profit.

Fair price is an important concept. You should work with your client to ensure that he or she understands that the fair price is a reflection of good business practice. It is not gouging; there is no excess profit involved. It is simply the fair value of the service that he or she wishes to acquire.

Having determined the fair price, you adjust it to reflect other factors. For example, you may be able to bid lower because your firm is located close to the client and transportation and travel costs will be minimal. Your past experience may also allow you to perform some of the tasks more efficiently than other firms. There may be some factors that make this job particularly important to your firm, in which case the price should be lowered to the degree that the importance dictates.

2. Approximate budget

You must not be shy about calling the client and asking what budget is assigned to the project and what significance is attached to the price. Often the client will not release the information. Do not let this deter you. Continue to probe with questions such as the following:

- What is the ballpark level of effort that you envisage?

- How important is price in this bid?

- Is price or quality more important to you?

3. Price relative to quality

If quality is at the top of the client's agenda, then your strategy is quite straightforward. Your concern then becomes to demonstrate that your firm can do the best technical job and you simply propose the fair price required to do it. You may even be able to add a surcharge if your firm can deliver a superior product or if some extra effort is required such as expert testimony or overtime.

If the client reveals the budget that is available, you would price the job accordingly. The client's budget may or may not be similar to the fair price. If it differs you may have to adjust the scope of work to reflect the client's budget.

The most difficult situations arise when price is an important factor to the client and will play a major role in determining the winning bid. In this case, you must be competitive and may have to bid considerably below the fair price.

4. Competition

The situation is exacerbated when there are a large number of bidders and when economic times are not very good. In these situations, you may need to reduce your margins substantially. A knowledge of how your competitors respond to such situations is critical.

The electronic age has been a boon to smaller businesses, allowing them access to many powerful tools through computer and electronic technology. These firms operate with very low overhead and can submit extremely competitive bids. Occasionally even larger firms will decide that they will pursue a contract at all costs, even if they have to take a loss. You face an uphill battle if there are some notorious low-ball artists among your competition. You must try to recognize these situations; analyze the RFP from the point of view of your competitors. Get to know how your competitors respond to these situations. Your pricing must reflect a balance between how low is economically practical and what you feel it will take to win.

Price is the single most important factor in a proposal and the most difficult to determine.

Times will arise when you should not submit a bid, even though your firm may have the best technical expertise, because you simply cannot match the low bids. In these cases, it is best to save your resources and hope that the tactics of your competitors will eventually lead them to bankruptcy.

If circumstances are such that you feel you must submit a proposal even though you know you are competing against notorious low-ball firms, the key is to submit a very simple bid. In essence, you are playing their game. With this approach, the overhead costs you save by avoiding an elaborate proposal can be transferred into the lower price.

In addition, cut your scope of work to the bare minimum that is responsive to the RFP. If you win the contract, you must be very careful only to perform the services that were specified. And if you lose the bid, you have not invested very much in the proposal preparation.

5. Importance to your firm

Always consider the importance of the project to your firm. The more important the job, the more you will want to compete. The bid-or-not-to-bid form shown in chapter 2 will help you make objective decisions.

Once the overall importance to your firm is established, then the price can be set accordingly. Of course, you must take into account other factors such as competition.

d. Write simply

The proposal must look neat and be professionally assembled. Fortunately, this is not difficult to achieve with modern word processing and desktop publishing tools. Even a small firm has the capability to produce attractive proposals with graphics and a professional layout.

Clarity and simplicity are of utmost importance in a proposal. By making the evaluator's job easy, you are doing him or her a favor which may not be quantifiable but is still very real. You have created a situation of indebtedness which is a very powerful psychological motivator.

Your proposal must stand out from the crowd.

The use of a simple and easy-to-follow style also builds technical credibility with the reader. After all, you have been able to explain a complex subject in an understandable manner. This must mean that you understand the subject.

Style and presentation is discussed in detail in chapter 5.

e. Add unique selling points

Your proposal must stand out from the crowd; it needs something unique so that the evaluators will notice it and select it from the many others that have been submitted. This is fundamental to winning competitive bids. These unique characteristics are termed unique selling points, or USPs, and they are recognized as being of critical importance to persuasion. They are also known by other words and terms such as the "wow factor," and "sparkle, snap, and pizzazz."

Your USPs are an important factor in the go or no-go decision. If you decide to proceed, you will need to sprinkle the USPs throughout the proposal. You must shout out the USPs! Insert them in the cover letter, introduction, and appropriate technical sections. You might consider including a closing summary section listing the USPs again.

Some examples of USPs include —

- Cheapest price

- Local presence

- Numerous offices

- Best technology in North America

- Unrivalled expertise in the country

- Greater backup/resources/reliability

- Sensitivity to social/environmental/cultural issues

- Some specific technology that is particularly applicable or cost efficient

If you feel that you have no particular USPs of a technical or cost nature, then perhaps you can introduce some innovative slants to your proposal. Perhaps a specially designed cover with a photograph or a graphic representation relevant to the project will make your proposal the most attractive. Now is the time to be innovative. Seek input from others in the firm with fertile spirit and wide-ranging imagination; use a "think tank" approach to develop your USPs.

f. Go the extra mile

One of the most powerful influence motivators is indebtedness. How can you create this with your client? The answer is "going the extra mile" and providing some extra service that your competitors do not.

Make a trip to visit the client's office or project site, even though this was not stipulated in the RFP. Learn about the project. Obtain background information that was not provided in the RFP. Meet the people behind the RFP. At the same time, you will have the opportunity to present an overview of your firm. The client will appreciate that you took the time to visit and prepare thoroughly for the proposal.

One example of extra effort is putting nicely designed covers on a proposal rather than just a standard cover. The cover should reflect the theme of the project that is being considered. One time my firm was bidding on an environmental cleanup project for an old railway site. We came across an historical photograph of the site and designed a very attractive cover showing an old locomotive crossing the original railway trestle. The client was very impressed by the extra effort. Not only did we win the contract, but the client requested an extra copy of the cover, which was framed and now hangs in the lobby.

Often there are good opportunities if you can establish contact with a potential client before the RFP is issued. Ideally you would use your powers of persuasion to convince him or her to issue the contract directly to you without the complications and wasted time of a competitive bidding process. Even if he or she is committed to obtaining competitive bids, perhaps you can assist by providing guidance in preparing the RFP. Often the client is not knowledgeable in writing RFPs and welcomes assistance or ideas on how to structure it.

5
PACKAGING THE PROPOSAL

Remember always that your proposal is not competing for the Pulitzer Prize. Your goal is to strive for clarity. An elaborate writing style is not only difficult and time-consuming to produce but also counter-productive. The proposal evaluator desperately wants something that is straightforward and easy to follow.

Your proposal must make its points simply. Your strengths must be readily apparent; the reader should not have to search in a jungle of hyperbole and jargon. You are writing with power when the reader has to do a minimum of thinking to understand your message.

To understand the importance of clarity, let's follow a proposal through the evaluation process.

Your firm has just submitted a major proposal to the federal government. The contract is very important to your firm and to you personally. Your reputation as the firm's top proposal writer will be greatly enhanced if you can win this one.

You and your team have put considerable effort into writing this proposal. As always, you followed the concepts outlined in this book and you placed considerable emphasis on presenting the proposal in a clear and easy-to-understand fashion. The text was written in straightforward English and abundant tables and graphs were used to guide the reviewer. Of course, it didn't hurt that your firm has good experience in this field with some very well-qualified experts. In particular, you highlighted the information that was requested as part of the evaluation criteria.

Clarity is paramount.

However, these are competitive times and your largest and fiercest rival has also submitted a strong proposal, as have a number of other firms. The government department responsible for the RFP, to show its "fairness," is using a very complex contractor selection process. There are five reviewers and they are using a predetermined set of evaluation criteria. Unknown to you, your efforts in preparing the proposal have paid off and your firm and your major competitor are in a virtual tie, with a clear lead over the other 13 bidders.

It appears that your rival has slightly greater technical depth, but your proposal has shown a more organized approach to the problem. At this stage, four of the reviewers have completed their evaluation and the review is in the hands of the fifth evaluator who has, in effect, the tie-breaking vote.

The fifth evaluator is Dave, and he is not a happy camper. Dave is no longer in the department that is sponsoring this contract, but he has been "volunteered" to participate in the review by his new boss because he owes some favors. Dave is struggling to adapt to his new department and is considerably behind in his work load. Furthermore, he has been having some personal difficulties on the domestic front where his teenage daughter has just brought home a failing report card, and he and his wife have also found themselves in debt. His banker has called him twice that week to suggest they get together to discuss this matter.

In spite of these problems and his busy schedule, Dave has managed to set aside this afternoon to review the 15 proposals. However, he is not in a good mood and his mind occasionally wanders to some of his personal problems. About halfway through the afternoon he reaches the proposal of your main rival. This team is very strong and, although you have also assembled a very competent project team, your rival's team is unquestionably stronger. However, the rival team was somewhat overconfident and left the proposal writing almost entirely to its top expert. This person has an internationally renowned reputation, but lacks proposal writing skills. The proposal reads like a scientific treatise and is accompanied by numerous citations and considerable technical jargon.

Although Dave struggles to follow the complex scientific reasoning, and although he is most impressed by the technical knowledge, he becomes noticeably irritated when the written text describing the technical approach does not match the accompanying flowchart. With difficulty he searches through the proposal to find the information he needs to complete his evaluation.

The next proposal Dave tackles is yours. He is pleasantly surprised that you have kept the use of technical jargon to a bare minimum, and the headache he has been nursing almost disappears when he finds you have summarized your team's strengths against each of the evaluation criteria, as well as cross- referenced each criterion to the relevant part of the text.

Dave is able to easily complete the evaluation. He finds the tabs a great help in moving through the proposal and is also impressed by the clarity of the presentation and how most of the main points are complemented by diagrams or tables. He is understandably relieved and thankful that his job has been made easy for him in his difficult time. It is not surprising that he gives your proposal the winning mark, even though at the back of his mind he has the gnawing feeling that perhaps your archrival's team is stronger.

It must be stressed that Dave is not an exceptional case. All of us have many activities and many concerns that preoccupy us. It is indeed a rare person that would be totally carefree and could devote undivided attention to reviewing a proposal. For this reason, your proposals should be written as though you expect Dave to be the reviewer every time. You can be assured that Dave will be grateful...and his evaluation marks will reflect it!

What are some of the techniques that you can use to make Dave's life easier?

- Avoid jargon or other complex wording that might not be understood. Remember, some members of the evaluation team may come from departments that are not directly involved in the project and may not be familiar with the subject area.

- Use lists when presenting a number of items or points rather than stringing them into long sentences. Lists are visually much easier to comprehend.

- Use tabs to separate main sections of your proposal. This is particularly helpful if your proposal is large. It makes it much easier for the evaluator to find, for example, the price section or the resumes.

- Use summary tables whenever possible. For example, use tables to list your previous jobs or your key staff and their primary expertise. An example of such a summary table is shown in Sample #3.

- If the RFP has specified the criteria to be used in evaluating the proposals, your concluding section should briefly discuss each criterion and outline how you satisfy it. If possible, a summary

SAMPLE #3
SUMMARY TABLE
(Showing education, expertise, and responsibilities of project staff)

Person	Degree(s)	Expertise	Responsibility
Joanne Smith	B.Sc. 1967 M.Sc. 1969 Ph.D. 1972	Waste Management	Project Manager
Ian Bill	B.E. 1962 B.Sc. 1964 Ph.D. 1967	Waste Management Water Resources	Technical Advisor
Bovine Blunt	B.A. 1975 M.Sc. 1980	Hydrogeology Site Remediation	Project Coordinator
David Chant	B.Sc. 1968 Ph.D. 1973	Risk Assessment	Risk Assessment
Christina Clark	B.Sc. 1984 M.Sc. 1986 Ph.D. 1990	Risk Assessment Chemical Fate Modelling	Risk Assessment
Don Hall	B.A.Sc. 1973	Geotechnical Engineering, Site Remediation	Site Remediation
Ron Hanna	B.Sc. 1983	Health & Safety	Health & Safety
Hank Hart	B.Sc. 1976	Environmental Assessment	Regional Coordinator
Betsy E. Cook	Eng. Tech. M.B.A. 1982	Field Engineering Administration	Field Support Administration
Bob Weiss	B.Sc. 1975 M.Eng. 1979	Geotechnical Engineering	Regional Coordinator Site Remediation

table should be included. The objective is to provide the reviewers with a single place from which they can complete their evaluation forms.

- Don't repeat lengthy sections from the RFP; refer to them.
- Don't throw everything into the proposal; you must avoid this pitfall.

    I recently reviewed a proposal for providing technical advisory services to a small town in rural North Dakota. The objective was to provide a source of technical expertise to the community so that they could independently monitor and assess a major project that was being constructed by the federal government.

    The consultant had prepared a 14-page statement of qualifications, even though the request had specified that it should be kept to ten pages or less. Furthermore, a substantial amount of space was devoted to describing the consultant's Canadian and overseas operations and experience. Although the firm was obviously proud that its operations were international in nature, this had absolutely no bearing on the project. In fact, the large international conglomerate image would be a negative factor to a small rural community or, at best, would cause uncertainty and confusion. The rest of the bid was in a similar vein, concentrating on describing at great length how great the firm was, rather than focusing on what the client wanted and illustrating how the firm's experience related to what the community needed. The bid did not make the short list.

- Neatness is a necessary component. You quickly destroy your credibility if the proposal is sloppy or if it contains abundant typographical errors. How can you be entrusted with the client's very important project if you are incapable of preparing and proofreading a neat proposal? Fortunately, most word processing packages include a spell checker which should correct most of the typographical glitches. The rest you will have to find by doing some proofreading. Take the extra hour or two that is needed for this chore.

- Beware of logic gaps. This is a common pitfall, particularly with inexperienced writers. Logic gaps include, for example, listing seven tasks in the text and showing only six in the flowchart, or giving the tasks different names in the text than in the schedule or flowchart. They distract the readers from their objective (evaluating your proposal) and instead force them to spend time deciding what is meant. Logic gaps are like typographical errors, only worse; they waste the reader's time and destroy goodwill and credibility.

Often the main or only product of the consulting project is the final report, which your proposal is a precursor to. It is only natural for the proposal evaluator to assume that the very important final report will be no better written than your proposal. Therefore, you must organize and write the proposal to a high standard. Sloppiness, typographical errors, poor layout, and inconsistent logic are not acceptable. Above all else, make it easy to understand.

6
THE BUILDING BLOCKS

This chapter returns to the basics. The fundamental elements, or building blocks, of a proposal are described. In addition, this chapter discusses how the persuasion guidelines discussed in previous chapters can be combined to produce a powerful and persuasive proposal.

The basic components of a proposal should be listed in the table of contents. An example of a contents page is shown in Sample #4. Each component of the table of contents is described below.

a. Cover letter

Although the cover letter is generally written after you have finished all the other components of the proposal, it is the first item seen by the recipient and it forms the opening salvo of your offensive to gain the reader's trust and support. Your cover letter should be brief and straightforward, indicating what you are submitting. The same letterhead and style should be used as for your firm's regular letters. Sample #5 shows a typical cover letter.

This is an important opportunity to briefly state the main strengths of your bid. The key unique selling points that differentiate your bid from the competing bids should be emphasized.

Close your cover letter on a cordial note. By adding warmth and a personal touch to the letter, you put the reviewers in a receptive frame of mind. A good way of achieving the personal touch is to liberally sprinkle the letter with "I" and "you." This technique adds personality and makes a positive and personal connection between your proposal and the reviewers. This is particularly effective if you have met the reviewers at some earlier stage.

SAMPLE #4
TABLE OF CONTENTS FOR A PROPOSAL

Cover Letter

Cover/Title Page

Proprietary Notice

Table of Contents

1. Introduction

2. Technical Approach

     - Objective(s)

     - Methodology

3. Project Team

     - Corporate Team

     - Project Team

4. Relevant Experience

5. Budget

6. Schedule

7. Certifications

8. Evaluation Criteria

Appendixes

A   - Corporate Descriptions

B   - Project Descriptions

C   - Resumes of Key Staff

Purchasing Department   July 6, 200-
Acme International Inc.
11 Laurier Street
Hullava, SC 10234

Dear Ms. Beasley:

<u>Proposal for a Health & Safety Training Program</u>

We are pleased to enclose four copies of our proposal for "A Company-Wide Health and Safety Training Program" in response to your request for proposal dated June 25, 200- (Your Reference: AFG-234).

As you will see, Quandary International has formed a strong project team with considerable expertise in all the main areas specified in your request for proposals, namely in toxicology, fire fighting, and personal protective equipment.

In particular, we have provided exactly such training before and have included a list of references from satisfied customers. As we are the only major training company that has offices located in the same cities as your branches, we can offer cost savings.

I would like to stress that Quandary has made a corporate commitment to this undertaking. Please do not hesitate to contact me if you should have any queries. I am very much looking forward to working with you and your colleagues.

Yours truly,

Pat Lane
Vice President

Quandary International Inc.
2345 Peabody Drive
Washington, DC 10123

Have the most senior person possible sign the cover letter, as this shows the commitment of your firm to the proposal.

b. Cover/title page

The cover and title pages are essentially the same. You should develop a standard format that is graphically appealing and can be produced efficiently. The cover should be laminated and can contain color. The title page would then be black and white and contain the identical, or very similar information as the cover.

The cover/title page is an interesting study in contrast. On the one hand it is simple and short, yet on the other hand, since it is one of the first components of your proposal that the readers see, it can be profoundly persuasive in its ability to form a strong and lasting impression.

The cover/title page has four components: the title, the name of the client or recipient of the proposal, the name of your firm, and the date. Note that the name of the client is usually at the top whereas your firm is listed at or near the bottom. This indicates your client-oriented approach; that is, you are proposing to improve the client's business, not selling your service.

The title should clearly state the proposal name without being too lengthy. However, seek ways to state the title in a positive, client-oriented manner, rather than just echoing a bland description from the RFP. For example, "Proposal to Improve Energy Efficiency at the Chicago Plant" is better than "Proposal for a Study of Energy Usage at the Chicago Plant."

Other information such as the client's file or reference number may be included. This can be useful for large clients who issue many RFPs.

You may wish to add some simple graphics to enhance the visual appeal of the title page. However, the graphics should not be too elaborate or detract from the main message. A small tip: always put on the cover the date the proposal is due, even if you plan to submit it earlier. This will allow you to get the cover production initiated right away.

The appearance of the proposal is a reflection of the quality of the report that you would produce. The appearance of the proposal can be a significant factor in the evaluation, especially in consulting where the final report is often the main product. For particularly large and important proposals, you should consider designing a unique cover that reflects the theme of the proposal.

A standard title page is shown in Sample #6.

c. Proprietary notice

An optional consideration is a proprietary notice warning the client that the information contained in the proposal is confidential and is to be used solely for the purpose of evaluating the proposal and is not to be disclosed to anyone outside the evaluation group without your written authorization. This notice should be used when you have confidential data, innovative ideas, or other information in your proposal that you do not want falling into the hands of your competitors. It can be very frustrating to lose the bid, but have the winning consultant use your brilliant concepts in the subsequent work. A good place for the proprietary notice is on the inside of the front cover.

d. Introduction

The main purpose of the introduction is to gently lead into the subject, rather than jumping in cold. You should also use this opportunity to give the reader confidence in the service or product that you are presenting.

The introduction should provide a brief summary of the background to the project in question, outlining the need for the service or product. It can also include a brief summary of what is to follow in the remainder of the proposal. You should highlight the key points that make your firm well suited for providing it. It is particularly important to include as many of your USPs in the introduction as possible. The readers/evaluators of your proposal should not have to search for your unique selling points; they should shine like beacons, guiding the reviewers to the correct conclusion — that your proposal is the best one.

You will find the introduction easy to write if you wait until the rest of the proposal has been completed. However, I prefer to write the introduction at the outset. It forces me to develop the USPs, become familiar with the background to the project, and thoroughly understand the objectives. The introduction also serves as a useful source of information for other staff who may be assisting in the proposal preparation.

Finally, the introduction should be kept short and sweet; I generally try to keep it to less than two pages.

Acme International Inc.
11 Laurier Street
Hullava, South Carolina

A Proposal for a
Company-Wide Health and Safety
Training Program

(RFP No. AFG-234)

July 200-

Quandary International Inc.
Washington, DC

e. Technical approach

This section allows you to reinforce your authority as an expert by laying out a sound technical plan for the project. The technical approach must demonstrate that you understand the problem and have a methodology for resolving it. This is the time to introduce innovative ideas or solutions. Your impact will be greatly lessened if the plan is fuzzy or general in nature, as invariably happens if you haven't taken the time to thoroughly research the subject. The methodology must be described including the resources that will be required.

The objectives, that is, the goals of your proposed effort, should be set forth at the beginning of this section. The objectives help arouse the readers' appetite because it tells them how they will benefit. If there is more than one objective, list them in the order of their importance to the client.

The more professionally you present the technical approach, the more competent you will appear and the more confidence the evaluator will have in your proposal. Brainstorming with some of your best technical experts is a useful way of gaining an understanding of the problem and developing a sound methodology. Innovative approaches should be sought and any unique selling points that your team can bring to the project should be highlighted.

Subdivide the project into tasks. The success of even the most complex projects undertaken by humankind is made possible because they are divided into small, manageable units. The hierarchy of tasks may vary from a few for small projects to many hundreds or even thousands of tasks and subtasks for more complicated projects such as the design of a linear accelerator or a nuclear power plant safety system.

A task must be measurable and assignable. That is, you should be able to assign a single person, the task leader, to be responsible for its execution, although other staff may also contribute to it. In addition, each task should have a definite outcome, a budget, and a duration. In other words, a task is a work element that can be assigned, have its progress monitored, and produce discrete deliverable components.

Examples of typical tasks are the following:

- Review literature on underground mining in Bolivia
- Compile data on investment opportunities for financial institutions in Mexico
- Test three materials for thermal conductivity

Reinforce your authority as an expert.

- Review previous site investigations for a cleanup project
- Perform additional site investigations to fill gaps in previous work

These are not tasks:

- Identify gaps in data (this is a result which might, for example, emerge from the fourth task listed above)
- Perform project efficiently (this is an objective)
- Hold initial meeting

If the project is at all complex, a flowchart of the technical approach will help the reader. It is a road map and should guide the reviewer through the technical network of your proposed methodology. The flowchart is often very helpful to you, as well, as its preparation forces you to analyze the logical flow and interrelationship of the technical tasks that you are proposing. A typical flowchart is shown in Figure #1.

A section on anticipated difficulties is generally helpful as it shows you have taken the time and interest to analyze potential problems and to think of ways of overcoming them. If the project has a particularly difficult schedule or budget to satisfy, then the effort you have invested in recognizing these obstacles and thinking about their resolution will gain the client's respect.

The technical approach is generally the longest section in your proposal and should certainly be the one that consumes the deepest thought.

f. Project team

This section presents your project team to the reader. If you have subconsultants on the team, you will want to include a simple corporate team organization chart. (An example is shown in Figure #2.) It is generally useful to include the name of the key coordinator for each organization.

In addition you can include a brief corporate overview of your firm and each of the subconsultants. This should be relatively brief so it does not distract the reviewers from their main mission. Do not forget to include any particular strengths or USPs. If the client is new and you feel more information is necessary, additional corporate boiler plates can be placed in one of the appendixes.

The main purpose of this section is to introduce the reader to the project staff. A project organization chart is a valuable tool and

FIGURE #1
TECHNICAL TASKS FLOWCHART

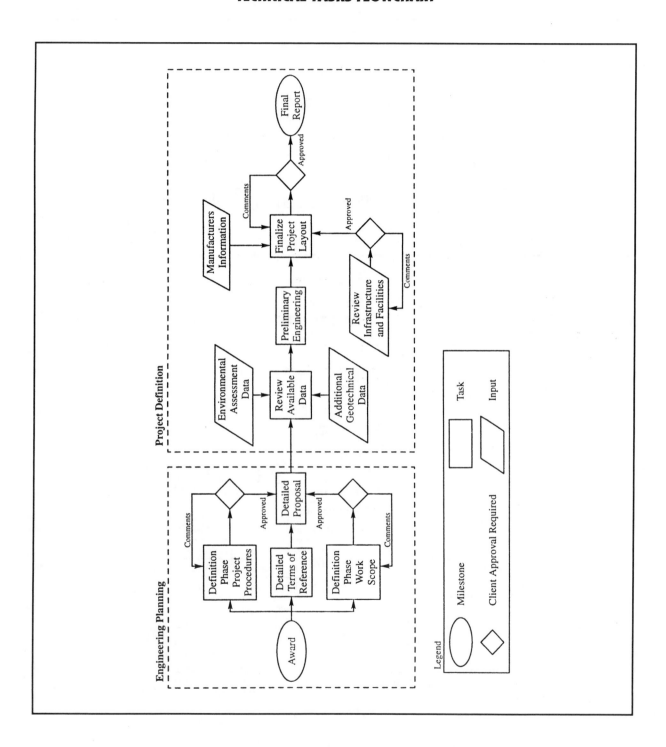

FIGURE #2
CORPORATE TEAM ORGANIZATION CHART

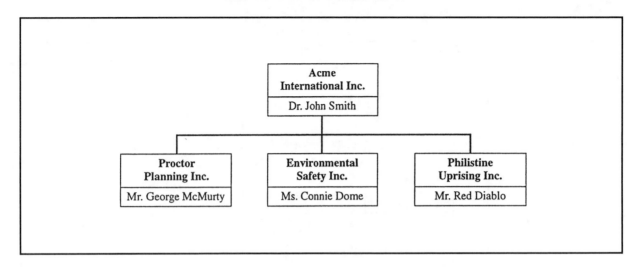

FIGURE #3
PROJECT ORGANIZATION CHART

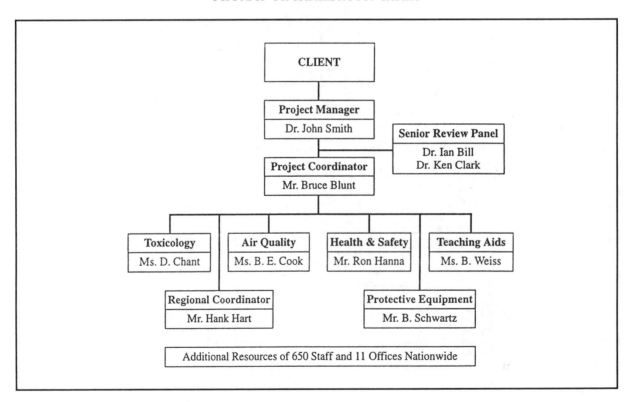

shows at a glance the hierarchy that you will use and the individuals involved. A typical project organization chart is shown in Figure #3.

For the key staff you should provide a brief capsule resume that describes the person's qualifications for this project and also the responsibilities he or she must assume. You should take the trouble to customize the capsule resumes so they specifically address the needs of this project, rather than just using the standard ones in your file.

Special emphasis should be placed on the project manager because he or she is the key technical person as well as the main conduit of communications between the project team and the client. You should strive to paint your project manager as a demigod who has most if not all of the following traits: authoritative in the subject under consideration, excellent verbal and written communication skills, clout within your organization, strong organizational skills, and a track record of successful projects.

Ensure that the project manager is placed in the best light possible.

g. Relevant experience

Your description of relevant experience is a vitally important part of the proposal. This section must establish the qualifications of your team and must forge a strong sense of confidence that your team has the technical and organizational expertise to perform the project. The bulk of the section should consist of capsule descriptions of relevant projects that your firm has performed. Lengthier descriptions should be placed in an appendix. Magazine articles, conference papers, or other publications are particularly effective in establishing your technical credentials and they should be summarized in this section. Occasionally, copies of the complete papers should be included in an appendix.

In addition, you should specify relevant equipment, facilities such as laboratories or computers, information sources such as data bases, and any other factors that show you can fulfill the technical requirements of the project and/or which provide you with an advantage over your competitors.

Quote similar or larger projects that you have successfully performed for other clients who are in the same field as the issuer of the RFP. As you will recall from chapter 3, this plays on the "social copying" principle of persuasion and is a very powerful motivator. You should also consider including the names and telephone numbers of a few references, even if the RFP has not requested this information.

Avoid discussing your rivals' weaknesses — such a tactic generally backfires. Instead, highlight your own strengths; a good evaluator will be able to draw the proper comparisons.

In spite of the importance of this section, it should not consume a great deal of your proposal preparation time. Most of the information can be drawn directly from files of relevant project descriptions in an appropriate word processing format which you have compiled expressly for the purpose of preparing your proposals efficiently. (The important topic of efficiency is discussed in more detail in chapter 7.)

h. Project budget

Your proposed budget is the single most important part of your proposal. Every other part of your proposal is qualitative, but the budget is quantitative and can be summarized in a single number. The strategy that you should employ in deciding how to establish that all-important number was discussed in chapter 4.

There are two basic kinds of price that can be proposed. The first is a fixed-price contract in which a single price is quoted. Your service will cost the client that exact amount. If you can do the work for less, then you will gain; if it costs you more, then the client will be the winner. This kind of contractual arrangement is often preferred by a client when there is some element of risk involved in the project. A firm price removes the risk for the client. The fixed price may be paid in one lump sum on completion of the project or payments may be paid on completion of certain milestones, with the remainder due when the job is done.

The other kind of contract, and the more common one, is where the cost of services is given a ceiling. Here, you are only paid for the amount of work that you perform, up to the specified ceiling. This kind of contract is used when there is some uncertainty about how much effort is required. It offers protection to the consultant in the event the work scope is not well defined or if there are unforeseen developments. Usually, billings are made at the end of every month for the labor and expenses incurred.

Regardless of the type of contract, you will need to perform a budget analysis. The client will usually want a detailed breakdown of your budget estimate. The cost for each of the following cost categories should be estimated:

- Labor
- Outside services (i.e., laboratory analyses)

- Travel

- Equipment

- Supplies

- Communications (e.g., long distance telephone, courier, fax)

- Subconsultants

- Miscellaneous

- Contingency

This kind of budget estimating is well suited to computer spread-sheet software. You should have a standard template for performing these cost estimates efficiently. For the labor cost, you could provide a table of the key staff, each person's hourly charge rate, and the number of hours each person will spend on the project. It is also useful to provide a table that is subdivided by task so that the total cost per task is shown.

A typical budget spreadsheet is shown in Figure #4. Note that this spreadsheet shows your in-house labor in detail. However, disbursements and subconsultant costs are only summarized. The data for these two categories can be calculated by hand or, better yet, obtained from separate spreadsheets. These other spreadsheets could be linked to the primary one so the key numbers come into it automatically. This spreadsheet method of estimating project costs for proposals is virtually mandatory as it allows hours and other costs to be juggled, changed, or deleted without having to recalculate the totals manually.

This spreadsheet is helpful for both the client and your project team as it presents costs broken down in several useful categories. The client can readily see how the resources are allocated and which tasks are receiving priority. This format is also a valuable planning aid once you win the contract. Each task leader can easily see who is assigned to the task and how many hours are allocated. Each person can also see the total hour commitment to this project and can integrate this information with the other project requirements.

In some cases you may not want or need to provide all of the information in Figure #4 to the client. Instead, you may wish to extract only the key data and present it as a separate table. An example of such a summary table is shown in Sample #7.

The fixed fee or the ceiling price should be clearly shown; under no circumstances should the reader have to search for these key numbers. It will aid the reader if there is a summary table, such as

FIGURE #4
BUDGET SPREADSHEET

Example Budget Spreadsheet by Task and Staff

	H. Tammeguchi		K. Askwood		D. Powder		J. Wizkid		Secretarial		Drafting		G. Penney		A. Ego	
Base hourly rate:	$38.00		$30.65		$33.58		$25.00		$15.00		$22.00				$90.00	
Full hourly rate:	$98.80		$79.72		$87.31		$65.00		$39.00		$57.20		$22.00		$57.20	
Task	hours	$	hours	$	hours	$	hours	$	hours	$	hours	$	hours	$	hours	$
1. Literature Review	4	395	10	797	6	524		0		0		0		0	12	1080
2. Churchill Falls	4	395	8	638	8	698		0		0		0	16	1440		0
3. LG-2	4	395	12	957	8	698		0		0		0		0	8	720
4. Field Work	12	1186	16	1275	80	6985		0	40	1560	8	458		0		0
5. Data Compilation	18	1778	32	2551		0	48	3120		0		0		0		0
6. Computer Analyses	2	198		0		0	6	390		0		0	24	2160	24	2160
7. Report	40	3952	16	1275	24	2095		0	40	1560	24	1373		0	4	360
8. Final Meeting	12	1186	12	957		0		0	4	156	2	114	12	1080		0
Totals	96	9485	106	8450	126	11000	54	3510	84	3276	34	1945	52	4680	48	4320

<----- Subconsultants ----->

Task Totals

	Labor (In-house)		Disbursements	Sub-Consultant	Total
	hours	$	$	$	$
	20	1,716		1080	2,796
	20	1,731		1440	3,171
	24	2,050		720	2,770
	156	11,464	3,400	0	14,864
	50	4,329	500	2160	6,989
	50	3,318	1,250	2160	6,728
	150	10,645	300	360	11,305
	30	2,413	940	1080	4,433
	0	0		0	0
	500	37,666	6300	9000	53,056

Sample #7, which lists each of the cost categories with their estimated budget. Other summary tables might also be included.

If it has not been specified in the RFP, it is important that you tell your future client how you expect to be paid. The payment method depends on a number of factors such as the nature of your business, your relationship with the client, your cash-flow position, etc. One common method is to request payment on a monthly basis, with your invoice submitted shortly after the month end. Another common method of payment is based on milestones, that is, certain fractions of the payment are released by the client as you reach specified milestones in the project.

In some cases when the project is of a relatively short duration, a single payment on completion of the project may be appropriate. Alternatively, if the client is a new one, or one whose credit-worthiness is suspect, you may wish to collect all or some of your fees in advance. Because of the large variation in how the payments can be made, it is essential that an understanding be established in advance and that you clearly note your preference in the proposal.

Cash flow is the life blood of all businesses. Thus, it is worthwhile to encourage your client to pay quickly. Your proposal should define the terms of payment that you expect and the penalty if those terms

SAMPLE #7
COST SUMMARY TABLE

	Hours	Cost ($)
Labor	500	37,666
Subconsultants	100	9,000
Disbursements	-	6,390
Total	600	53,056

are not met. For example, you might specify that your invoice is due within a certain period of its receipt, say 30 days, or you might request that payment be issued immediately upon receipt of the invoice. In either case, you may also wish to include a statement that a penalty of, say 1.5% per month, will accrue to overdue accounts.

i. Schedule

The timetable for the project is specified in some detail in the schedule section of your proposal. One of the best ways to convey the schedule to the reader is to develop a diagram that shows:

(a) each task as a function of time,

(b) the interrelationships between tasks (i.e., can task #3 begin only when task #2 has been completed, or can it be done in parallel?),

(c) major meetings, and

(d) milestones.

These schedule diagrams are known as PERT diagrams. PERT stands for project evaluation and review technique, which is a formal method of investigating the logical sequence of tasks and resolving the order and time over which they should be performed. It is sometimes also called the critical path method. It is a common method used in planning and managing projects, particularly when they are large and complex, but also very useful in planning smaller projects. See Figure #5 for an example.

The schedule diagram will help you analyze the complexities involved in the project and identify potential problem areas. To recognize which tasks are critical and which could delay the project, you should define those tasks where any delay will cause a delay to the entire project. It is also important to identify where your resources may be stretched thin; for example, when there are several tasks being done in parallel. Most good computer project management software programs have the capability to show the time requirements by skill (i.e., labor category).

By identifying potential difficulties in the schedule and how you propose to overcome them, you are demonstrating to the client that you understand the problem. This will gain his or her confidence and trust — very important commodities — which you should relentlessly pursue.

FIGURE #5
PROJECT SCHEDULE

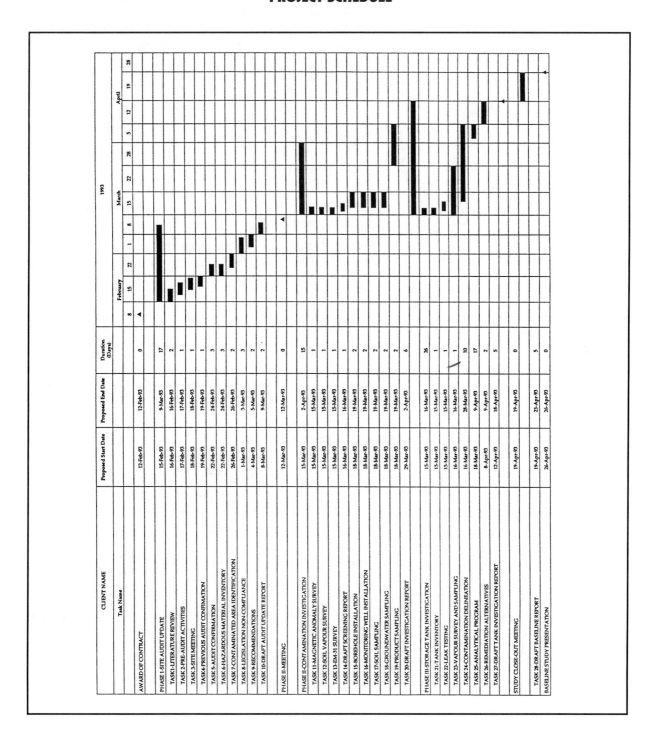

The client always has a strong interest in closely following the project to ensure that it will be completed on schedule and successfully. To help the client track your progress you can provide him or her with a set of milestones that should be clearly marked on the schedule diagram and also described in the text of the proposal.

The final date of completion of the project and the total duration should be clearly specified and should match the expectation of the client.

j. Certifications

With some proposals, particularly on government bids, various certifications are requested. These might include:

- Certification of the validity of the educational qualifications of the proposed staff

- Certification that none of the goods or services to be provided originates from countries the government does not do business with

- Certification that the price will remain valid for 90 days

- Certification that if your firm wins it will enter into a contract according to the terms specified in the attached contract document

- Certification that your firm has an employment equity program

If only one relatively brief certification is required, it might be included in the cover letter. However, if several certifications are involved, they should be placed into one section where they can be readily referenced. As certifications are necessary material that do not enhance your bid, this section should be placed in the appendixes or some other out-of-the-way section so it does not interfere with the important parts of your message.

k. Evaluation criteria (or why your firm should win this contract)

Close your proposal with a section that discusses the evaluation criteria. This serves three purposes. It simplifies the task of scoring your proposal for the evaluator, it ensures your proposal is complete and responsive to all the evaluation criteria, and most important, it highlights and emphasizes your key strengths and unique selling points. An evaluation summary table would be a useful supplement to your text and would graphically show that your proposal has addressed all the criteria. The readers will not only be thankful to you for making their job easier, but they will also close on a very positive note with all your good features fresh in their memories.

Often the RFP will not provide the criteria by which your proposal is to be evaluated. Never mind! In these instances you simply rename this section "Summary of Key Features of Proposal" and inundate the reader with the strengths of your bid relative to what you feel the evaluation criteria might be.

l. Appendixes

It is convenient to place some of your lengthier information in appendixes so it does not obscure the main message you are presenting. Typically, there are three standard appendixes. The first contains corporate descriptions of your firm and any subconsultants you may be using. This would include brochures. The second contains technical information regarding project experience such as descriptions of projects, copies of technical papers, lists of similar projects, etc. The third appendix contains resumes of the key staff. It will help the reader if these are arranged alphabetically and if the names of the individuals are listed on the appendix cover page.

m. Items to omit

You must bear in mind that although a proposal looks much like a report, it is quite different. First, your firm, not the client, pays for the proposal preparation. Furthermore, it is a task that you do frequently. Thus, it is essential that you minimize the effort involved, that is, the cost of preparation. One component of cost cutting is to omit any extraneous, unnecessary detail. Finally, unlike reports that remain as reference documents for many years, once the bid is evaluated the proposals are no longer used and become obsolete. In fact, all your proposals will wind up in the client's waste bin eventually. The losing ones just get there sooner.

Leave time for a final review.

Several items can be omitted from a proposal that would normally be included in a report. These include a list of tables, figures, and references. These items are all essential components of a report but can readily be omitted from a proposal; none of them will gain you marks with the proposal evaluators. For smaller proposals, the executive summary can also be omitted.

n. Final review

It is an unfortunate fact that proposals are almost always prepared in a mad rush to meet the submission deadline. You must do everything humanly possible to overcome the natural tendency to write the proposal at the last minute. Allow sufficient time to perform a thorough final review. This should be considered a formal part of the proposal preparation process. The reviewers should be coldly objective and should use the evaluation criteria specified in the RFP as their yardstick. In addition, do a careful final check of the RFP; it is remarkably easy, for example, to leave out a certification. A final proofread of the assembled document is also mandatory. It is amazing how often a figure is omitted or put in upside down. Make sure that nothing is overlooked.

You should take a final opportunity to go over the unique selling points, ensuring that they are clearly established and placed frequently and positively throughout the proposal. If possible, a knowledgeable person who was not involved in the proposal writing should perform this review.

Because of the overwhelming importance of price, you should perform a final evaluation to determine if your pricing strategy is satisfactory. Perhaps some new information has surfaced or the proposal preparation has given the opportunity to think more carefully about the strategy.

7
EFFICIENCY EQUALS PROFIT

For a consulting firm the proposal is the lifeblood of its business. Proposal preparation must be effective and efficient. This book stresses both factors: increasing the winning percentage and also improving the efficiency of the proposal preparation process. The bottom line is to increase revenue and decrease cost — two powerful ways for your firm to become more profitable.

This chapter explores the logistics of proposal preparation and how cost savings can be realized in the process. An essential part of the efficiency process involves standardization, a concept that made Henry Ford rich and famous. Another key ingredient is the computer, a powerful tool that takes away the drudgery of retyping and revising, and allows you to focus on the creative aspects of proposal preparation. In addition, we will discuss the people that run the production line and produce the high-quality, persuasive proposals.

Proposal preparation must be efficient.

a. What does it cost to prepare a proposal?

Before exploring how to make your proposal preparation more efficient, it's useful to examine the costs involved. For example, how does your organization allocate proposal budgets? Is it done by relying on previous costs, that is, using a historical approach? Do you have a formula for estimating the budget to be assigned to a specific proposal? Let's look at how a proposal budget might be calculated.

Your budget should be determined at the bid-or-not-to-bid decision-making stage. Some firms have rules of thumb for assigning a proposal budget. Generally, this is around 5% of expectation, where expectation is the product of the contract value, including indirect benefits, times the probability of winning the contract:

Proposal Budget = approximately 5% of Expectation

Expectation = Probability x (contract value + indirect benefits)

For example, if you are bidding on a $75,000 contract (with no indirect benefits) and you estimate that your chances of winning are 40%, you would allow a budget of $1,500 (5% of Expectation = 0.05 x .40 x $75,000).

However, this formula is only a guideline and should be modified to suit the needs of each specific proposal. For example, some firms do not include disbursements, such as subconsultant costs, in the contract value as these are only passed through and do not contribute to the revenue for the firm. There are many exceptions and each case needs to be considered on its own merits. The "5% of expectation" budget should be increased for small proposals as well as ones for the government, as these require greater effort. A smaller percentage would be allowed for large proposals and ones for private industry. If your firm deals primarily with larger contracts, you would need to tailor the formula to fit your specific situation, probably by decreasing the factor below 5%.

Be realistic in assessing how much the proposal preparation will cost. Some proposals can be excessively expensive and should be avoided.

Statistics can be a valuable guide in determining acceptable budgets for your proposals. You should rigorously keep statistics on the RFPs you receive and all the bids you submit. This information should be regularly reviewed to assess your win/lose percentage and the costs of your proposals. This data will not only let you know whether your win/loss ratio is improving, but also how the efficiency of preparing your bids is progressing, that is, whether the cost per proposal is decreasing. It will also let you set and adjust the "percentage of expectation" factor for allowing you to set proposal budgets that adequately reflect your firm and the business you are pursuing.

b. Standardize your proposal preparation system

Standardize! Standardize! Standardize! There is a mistaken belief that you need to write an original manuscript each time a proposal is submitted. This is completely false. You will not be penalized by an evaluator for reusing the same format, style, and even the same sentences that you have used in previous proposals. First of all, 99 out of 100 evaluators will not know that you are repeating material from previous bids. Furthermore, the evaluator doesn't care. He or she is totally preoccupied with looking for the information needed for evaluating the proposal. The evaluators simply want to get the job over and done with as soon as possible so they can return to other activities.

Standard templates for title page, cover letter, and introduction are a necessity. You should only need to change the project title, client name, and date. A few sentences in the cover letter and introduction would also need rewriting, but this should be kept to a minimum and should focus on your USPs.

You should develop a standard format and table of contents which is acceptable to most of your clients and which is flexible. It should contain most of the components described in chapter 6. This format may be influenced by government agencies, as they tend to have demanding and elaborate requirements. Whenever possible, you should retain the standard format. There are always exceptions, but these are easy to deal with once a standard format is established. You may want to develop a standard format for a shorter letter proposal as well.

All the sections should follow the same format. Only the technical approach and summary (or evaluation criteria) will require major original thought and writing. But even here the sequence and outline should follow your standard format. For the other sections you should be able to use the same basic figures for the schedule and organization chart each time but with the dates and names changed.

You should have a comprehensive library of standard boiler plate material that can be readily accessed and collated into your proposals. For example, capsule resumes of your key staff should be prepared. It is generally useful to have more than one on each person so that the proposal can be slanted toward particular topics. Similarly, capsule project descriptions should be kept on computer file.

In the technical approach, the tasks should be prepared and scheduled so that you can prepare a project budget from them with minimal fuss. The tasks need to be defined as quantifiable work packages with time and staff assigned to them. If you win the job, you should be able to take the work plan directly from your proposal

Develop a standardized approach for proposal preparation.

and input the information into your project planning forms. Prepare the budgets and labor schedules in exactly the same format as your organization uses in planning your projects. This approach will not save time in proposal preparation, but it will certainly save time in getting the project started when you win the contract.

Appendixes should also follow a standard format for every proposal. For example, I always have Appendixes A, B, and C contain corporate information, project descriptions, and resumes respectively. That way, other members of the proposal writing team can include references to the appendixes in the text as they write, rather than having to backtrack after everything has been completed to fill in the appendix numbers.

c. Computer technology

Computers are marvelous instruments. They can do mathematical manipulations, operations, and logical processes with amazing speed. They have had a fundamental influence on our society and the way we do many of our jobs, and writing is one of the fields which has been influenced the most. Not too many years ago we would have considered computers a convenience in preparing proposals; today they are absolutely essential!

The more the proposal preparation process is standardized and the more computers are used, the more time you will have for creative thinking. Firms maximizing the use of computers will prosper. As computer technology continues to evolve rapidly, the firms that find new ways to adapt leading edge technology to streamlining proposal preparation will be the winners.

Let's explore some of the ways that computers can make proposal preparation more efficient and more effective.

1. Data bases

It is essential to have a comprehensive proposal library on an electronic data base which is easily accessed. The library should include corporate boiler plate, resumes of staff, capsule resumes, lengthy and capsule project descriptions, and past proposals.

2. Word processing

In preparing the first draft of the proposal, put into use the "two document" mode on the word processor. That is, two documents should be loaded into memory: the template for the section you are writing that will become the final product, and the resource document, which may be a past proposal, project description, or resume.

Cut and paste from the resource document into the template to save time.

Most word processing packages also allow graphics to be readily incorporated into the text. Generally, pictures or diagrams greatly enhance the message you are trying to deliver and should be employed often. In addition to the standard organization charts and schedules, you should acquire a graphics library of icons to add zest to your presentation.

3. Local area network

A local area network (LAN) provides additional power to your proposal team, allowing them to communicate rapidly, to retrieve files from the library, and to exchange files. A network also allows all the written text to be stored on one central computer hard drive which greatly improves the ability to track and control revisions to the proposal.

One of the greatest frustrations is trying to control multiple copies of a proposal undergoing a series of revisions by different people. Using a network with a central storage of the proposal files will help alleviate this headache. By using a modem link into the LAN, some of your proposal team can be located in another office or even at home.

4. Spreadsheets

Spreadsheets are an indispensable tool for calculating and presenting your budgets. A standard spreadsheet template lets you perform the calculation rapidly, and makes the seemingly endless revisions (that are an inherent part of proposal costing) easy. Once the budget figures are finalized, the appropriate presentation-quality tables should be prepared by importing the data into your document.

5. The World Wide Web

The World Wide Web contains a storehouse of useful information for the resourceful proposal writer who knows how to search the electronic pathways. Chapter 2, section **a.**, describes how the Web can be used to obtain information on government and private sector RFPs. In addition, there are numerous companies that can provide assistance in preparing your proposal; there are others that specialize in obtaining government procurements; yet others market software for writing proposals. If you feel that any of these would be of assistance to you, use a search engine to search the World Wide Web using the key words, "business proposal."

Maximize the use of computer technology.

If you do not know much about a potential client who has just issued an RFP, scrutinize their company Web site; this is a valuable source of information that should not be overlooked. Web sites are also a useful place to find out about your competitors. And you do not have to leave the comfort of your office to do all this research!

d. The proposal team

People, not computers, write proposals. However, they do not always do so happily. Often the call for volunteers is met with a chorus of groans and excuses. Many people have a fear of proposal writing. This fear is rooted in many reasons, the majority of which are generally justified, for writing winning proposals is not an easy task. Proposals are often written under intense pressure. For example, there may be a very short period of time available, and beating the looming deadline requires overtime work that disrupts family and private life.

Some people may have a natural fear of the creative thinking required for winning proposals. It is only too easy to land head first into writer's block when a deadline hangs over your head. There may also be a fear of rejection should the proposal lose; this may be exacerbated by senior managers who may place considerable stress on the proposal team with a win-at-all-costs attitude.

However, there is also an excitement associated with proposal writing. There is creative thinking and challenge and competition. Nothing can beat the wonderful exhilaration when you learn that your proposal has won. And there is also the very important reward that comes with bringing in new business to your firm, in landing new clients, and in opening up new fields of endeavor.

Try to cultivate that atmosphere of excitement around the proposal preparation process and ensure that the proposal team is properly recognized within your organization and rewarded for its efforts. These people are key to the financial success of your firm.

It is also essential to instill an ethic of efficiency in those individuals who write proposals. Invest time in teaching your staff the standardized approach and format that you use. They will need to learn that speed is of the essence and that they cannot agonize over the nuance of a word. They must assemble the basic proposal quickly. Speed minimizes problems with deadlines, allows time for creative thinking, and reduces the cost of proposal preparation.

The proposal writing team should, whenever possible, include some of the people who will be involved in the project if you are

Avoid large proposal writing teams.

successful. This will allow the project to start quickly and efficiently since they are familiar with the details of what is to be done. In essence, this requires that a large number of your technical staff be familiar with how to write proposals.

A good proposal writer should possess three essential skills: technical knowledge, an understanding of the psychology of marketing (i.e., persuasion), and presentation skills such as writing, graphics, and layout. Because of the importance of the proposal, those individuals who combine the above traits are a valuable corporate asset. However, it is difficult to find all of these talents embodied in one person — a person who has the requisite technical knowledge generally has not acquired the last two skills as part of their formal education. Seek out those who have a natural ability for proposal writing; these people should be fostered and their skills augmented by further training.

The proposal manager, who coordinates the efforts of the proposal team, deserves special mention. The manager must have the three characteristics described above and a number of other important traits. He or she must have good organizational skills which will be sorely tried in keeping track of and pulling together the myriad details that must be dealt with under the pressure of the deadline. The manager must also have strong people skills and be capable of maintaining harmony throughout this stressful process. The manager must also be able to seek out and assimilate a wide range of ideas, so that no creative stone is left unturned in the quest to prepare a winner.

e. The proposal preparation process

To this point we have looked at the different components of a proposal, the underlying psychology of persuasion, the importance of standardizing the preparation process, and the types of people who would be involved in the proposal preparation team. Let's now draw these different factors together and look at the process that would be followed once an RFP arrives at your door. The process can be divided into six steps as discussed below.

1. Making the decision to bid

The first step is to make the bid-or-not-to-bid decision. This needs to be done quickly and objectively. The purpose is to identify your weaknesses, not to gloss them over, so they can be properly addressed in your proposal.

2. Selecting the team

The second step is to select the proposal manager and the proposal writing team. Overall efficiency and quality will be enhanced if the team is as small as possible. Large proposal teams should be avoided whenever possible because they are like committees and will quickly squander your budgets, run over schedule, and produce an inferior product. Remember, a hippopotamus is a horse that was designed by a committee. You want your proposal to be sleek and fast and to outrace the pack, rather than being cumbersome and ungainly.

The team members should have those special qualities that are needed to write persuasive proposals. Furthermore, there must be a management commitment to make these people available, without other interruptions or responsibilities.

3. Holding the initial meeting

The third step is to hold the initial meeting. This is a vitally important meeting and will have a major influence on the outcome of your proposal. You must ensure that all the details are properly dealt with because you won't have the time to easily recover from any omissions later.

Collecting ideas, gathering intelligence, and developing an overall strategy is an integral component of proposal writing. Involve a larger group for the initial brainstorming and strategy session. This will ensure that a broad range of ideas are tabled. However, once the meeting is over, have a small and compact writing team, ideally consisting of one to three people, prepare the proposal. Naturally, for very large proposals or when a proposal has to be prepared in a very short period of time, larger writing teams must be assembled.

Hold the initial meeting as soon as possible, preferably within a day or two of receiving the RFP. Here is an agenda of items that should be addressed at the initial meeting:

(a) Provide an overview of the RFP verbally and in writing. Some key people should receive a copy of the RFP prior to the meeting.

(b) Determine the technical approach that will be taken to provide the service or product in some detail. Resolve how you will provide what the client wants. This is one of the most important objectives of the meeting, for without knowing what you are going to do, you cannot designate a project team, prepare a schedule, or do the cost estimates. Due to the limited time you have, these cannot be left until later.

(c) Select a project team. It would be best if some of the project team were also on the proposal writing team as it leads to a smooth project startup if you win the bid.

(d) Select subconsultants if necessary. The technical weaknesses that were identified in the bid-or-not-to-bid stage now need to be strengthened. Subconsultants need to be selected to provide the appropriate expertise. If a subconsultant has a good reputation with the client and is reasonably close geographically, it generally adds value to the project team.

(e) Lead a session of intensive brainstorming on the unique selling points that your team has to offer. As discussed in chapter 3, it is critical that your bid stand out from the rest of the pack. Identify as many USPs as possible and rank them in importance. Put some thought into how they will be presented. The important USPs should be interspersed in the proposal in several places. They should be clearly and forcefully presented; the reader should not have to search for them or have to infer them from indirect statements. Do not overlook this step of identifying USPs.

(f) Identify any questions. Very seldom is an RFP so well written that no ambiguities are present. Gather the questions from the entire proposal team. Then the proposal manager should call and discuss these with the client's representative. This is a very positive step as it not only obtains the missing information, but also usually uncovers other useful facts. Most important, however, it builds personal bonds; human contact is one of the most powerful persuaders. For this reason you should seek reasons to call the client.

(g) Make writing assignments. Due to time constraints, the proposal manager must get as many people working in parallel as possible. An assignment chart such as the one shown in Sample #8 is useful to track progress and ensure that nothing is accidentally overlooked. Every person that receives an assignment must also receive a deadline. As stated earlier, there must be a management commitment so the assignees will have the time to perform their responsibilities.

The initial meeting is vitally important and will have a major influence on the outcome of your proposal.

SAMPLE #8
PROPOSAL ASSIGNMENT FORM

Proposal Name: Erie Canal Widening Project   Number: P0352

Proposal Manager: A. Greaves   Date: November 13, 200-

Due Date: November 30, 200-

Section	Person Responsible	Date Due	Draft #1	Final
Cover	Jones	November 16		
Cover Letter	Smith	November 19		
Executive Summary	Greaves	November 23		
1. Introduction				
2. Technical Approach				
3. Project Management				
4. Corporate Experience				
5. Schedule				
6. Cost				
7. Evaluation Criteria				
Appendix A: Corporate Overview				
Appendix B: Project Descriptions				
Appendix C: Resumes				

4. Performing the work

The fourth and most time-consuming task is to perform the work assigned in the initial meeting. The work consists of three parts:

(a) The subconsultants must be contacted and persuaded to join your team, rather than a competitor's. The subconsultants should also be requested to provide information for the proposal including resumes, summaries of relevant project experience, corporate boiler plate, hourly or daily labor rates, and written sections describing the technical tasks for which they are responsible.

(b) Each person on the proposal team must write the sections assigned to them. Their sections should be submitted on diskette. They can also use material from your library of corporate information.

(c) The proposal manager must combine the text created by the other team members and ensure that it reads in a coherent and persuasive manner.

5. Reviewing the draft

The fifth task is to review the draft proposal. All too often this step is omitted because time does not allow it. Do not fall into this trap! Careful scheduling can and will allow time for a review.

The review should be done by someone who was not involved in the proposal preparation, yet who is familiar with the technical subject and has good persuasive skills. This person should edit the document and make constructive changes, that is, actually rewrite the text, rather than making general statements such as "this is too vague" or "needs strengthening." The reviewer should work in close collaboration with the proposal manager and together they should collectively make revisions as the review is being done.

6. Submitting the proposal

The sixth and final step is to mass produce, bind, and submit the proposal. Quality control is important at this stage as it is very easy to inadvertently omit a figure or put it in the proposal upside down. Filing all the proposal materials is also important as there must be an easily traceable paper trail should you win the bid. All aspects of the cost estimate must be recorded and filed properly.

***

In summary, it is not only important to write persuasive proposals, it is equally important to write them quickly and efficiently. To achieve this goal you should standardize the proposal preparation approach, use computer technology to the maximum extent possible, and have a small, motivated proposal writing team.

8
PERSUASIVE MEETINGS

Proposals are seldom written in isolation. An integral part of the proposal preparation process is interaction with the client through meetings and telephone conversations. Meetings, in particular, allow you to reinforce your proposal in a powerful and persuasive manner.

Meetings concerning proposals may arise in a number of ways. Often, when the project is complex or large, the client arranges a pre-bid meeting prior to the submission date to explain the bid package and to answer questions. As well, for larger contracts meetings in the form of interviews are often held. In these cases, the interview forms part of the formal proposal process and usually is held after the written submissions have been received and evaluated.

Independent of the pre-bid meeting and the interview, which are associated with the proposal, you should always strive to arrange additional information meetings, preferably prior to the issue of any RFP. These can be arranged for a variety of reasons. For example, a meeting to view the client's operations offers an opportunity to seek clarification, introduce your team members, and describe your qualifications.

a. The importance of face-to-face meetings

Personal contact is one of the most powerful sales methods. Whenever possible, you should strive to arrange face-to-face meetings with your potential clients. You and your colleagues are unique and getting together with a potential client you can display your individuality and build a bond between you.

Personal contact is the best sales method.

Whenever you send written promotional information, no matter how persuasive the covering letter and enclosed material, it will either wind up in the wastepaper bin or, at best, only be briefly skimmed. The personal visit ensures that your message is received. In addition, it allows you to pass on the exact message you want to deliver while developing empathy.

Face-to-face meetings provide a trio of important opportunities that cannot be achieved through a written submission. First, a meeting is interactive. You can see and hear your client's reaction to your ideas and can respond accordingly. You can judge whether you are being received favorably, whether your proposal has met all of the requirements, and whether there are any specific concerns or misconceptions. The feedback you receive will allow you to reinforce certain technical aspects of your team or improve your corporate image or make any other adjustments necessary to ensure that the client is totally satisfied with your firm.

If you are in a pre-bid meeting, it is more difficult to make a strong impression because all the competing consultants are also present, and it is more of an information presentation by the client with no opportunity to interact on a personal basis. Nevertheless, take full advantage of the opportunity by learning as much as possible about the client's operation and the nature of his or her problems.

A meeting also presents you with the opportunity to ask questions and obtain information on your client's operation and approach to business. It is critically important that you exercise the right to probe and, more important, to listen. What you find out about the client may make the difference in how you develop your proposal. In other words, you can quietly glean the data you need to make a client-centered approach. As discussed earlier, this is a crucial factor in persuasion.

In addition to generally promoting your capabilities, you should solicit as much information as possible from the client regarding any forthcoming proposals. If there are some impending RFPs, you should strive to obtain that work on a sole-source basis. If that strategy is unsuccessful, the next tactic is to lay the groundwork so that your proposal will be the winning one.

A third opportunity is meeting the client's key staff in person, allowing you to establish a bond with them. Ask questions and take a sincere interest in them personally as well as their work. Natural warmth can develop from such direct human contact. Apply the persuasion principle of empathy. In addition, an understanding of their personalities may provide some direction as to how your proposal might be prepared and which aspects should be emphasized.

b. The interview

Clients use interviews to become more familiar with the short-listed firms and to seek further clarification of the proposals. Because the interview is usually the last thing done by the client before a decision is made, it leaves a strong impression and often is the deciding factor in the selection of the winning consultant.

The principles involved in taking part in an effective interview meeting can be applied, with some modification, to almost all situations where verbal persuasion is required. However, to provide a specific focus, the post-proposal submission interview is described here. This interview is usually held with the firms who have presented the best proposals in order to get a better feel for the project team and resolve some of the details. The interview is one of the most important meetings that you can attend with the client and, thus, it is essential that you are at your persuasive best.

A successful, persuasive interview can be divided into two separate components: the presentation which generally follows relatively formal lines, and a discussion period after the presentation where the client seeks further clarification. In addition, I suggest that you identify the preparation for the interview and the rehearsals as distinct tasks that form an integral part of the interview. A final task is to prepare a handout that can be left with the client. Thus, there are five discrete tasks or components to an interview:

(a) Preparing the presentation

(b) Rehearsing the presentation

(c) Making the presentation

(d) Taking part in discussion

(e) Preparing the handout

1. Preparing the presentation

In preparing your presentation you should largely echo your proposal. Describe your team's qualifications, outline the technical approach and schedule, and then respond to any specific questions that the client may have.

It is essential that you establish technical authority and credibility. You should also include all your unique selling points and other

Always remember the chemistry of personal contact.

key features of your bid. You should list these on slides or transparencies and discuss them. These are the factors that will sell your proposal and it is essential that you highlight them. In other words, your presentation simply outlines the same persuasion principles that were contained in the written proposal.

Remember to take a very strong client-oriented approach. Since you will be face to face with the client, it is very important that you show a sincere interest in his or her operations and problems. Take the time to weave an understanding of these concerns into your presentation, rather than just describing your team.

As in your proposal, clarity is essential. Avoid the trap of expounding at length. Keep your illustrations simple and avoid jargon.

During the preparation phase you should also prepare two lists of questions. One should contain all the questions you wish to ask the client. Make sure that you have plenty of questions. You need to know an enormous amount about the client's business and only a fraction of this will have been covered in the RFP. Furthermore, you need to establish empathy with the client and the best way to achieve this is to show an interest in his or her business. Prepare questions that may not relate directly to the proposal but may be of interest to you anyway.

The other list should contain the questions that you anticipate the client will ask your team. Be hard-nosed. Analyze where your weaknesses lie and expect the client to ask about them. Naturally, you will prepare responses that will allay the client's concerns.

2. Rehearsing the presentation

The appearance or packaging of the written proposal makes an important impression on the reader. You have taken some pains to ensure that the proposal has a top-notch, professional appearance. In the presentation, the impression comes from the physical appearance of you and your team members and how you convey yourselves.

Rehearse your presentation.

To ensure a favorable impression is made, you *must* rehearse your presentation; this task should not be taken lightly. Even professional speakers and actors practice their lines.

If you are uncomfortable with public speaking, you should seek advice from a book, from one of the better speakers in your firm, or from a club such as Toastmasters. There is only one way to still those butterflies when you rise to address an audience, and that is to practice, practice, and practice some more.

The audience for your rehearsal should be carefully selected individuals who will provide a constructive, no-holds-barred critique. Practicing what you prepare is not enough. You must seek out constructive criticism and make revisions to improve and strengthen the presentation. Depending on the importance of the project, you may wish to rehearse more than once, perhaps initially by yourself or with a small audience and subsequently with a larger group in a more formal setting.

A vital component of the rehearsal is preparing for the questions that you anticipate from the client. Make sure you include these in the rehearsal and that you are satisfied with the responses you give. The interactive part of an interview is the most difficult. Being very familiar with the subject helps, as does the ability to think on your feet. You should have people pose a number of unexpected questions to test and improve your skills.

The rehearsal also provides the opportunity to become familiar with the transparency projector, microphones, and other aids that you may be using. For best results, you should rehearse in a room that is similar to the one in which the interview will be held.

Project confidence.

You must project confidence! One of the most important purposes of a rehearsal is to ensure you deliver your presentation with poise and great conviction. To achieve this, you must believe in the service you are selling. The confidence in your message must be part of you and must permeate right into your marrow. You must *know* your message!

3. Making the presentation

The day of the interview has arrived. Your presentation has been prepared and rehearsed. You are well-groomed and neatly dressed in a business suit because you recognize the importance of establishing an authoritative presence.

The introductions are over and you begin the presentation. Avoid the common mistake of jumping into the technical details of your presentation too quickly. Introducing your subject slowly greatly assists your audience. You should discuss the background, objectives, and provide a frame of reference. Assist your audience by presenting an outline of what you are going to say at the outset. You should proceed through the main topics in a clear and logical progression. Be sure to have clear introductions to, and transitions between, any new topics that you discuss.

It always helps to start with some pleasantries or humor. Humor is a powerful ally in alleviating boredom and keeping the audience alert. It will also help keep you relaxed. However, canned or forced humor can detract from the quality of your presentation. If you are not comfortable with introducing humor, don't.

Your objective is not only to lead into your presentation gently, but also to establish empathy with the audience. The first minute or two of your presentation are the most important, so make sure that this part goes well, even if it requires memorization.

As discussed earlier, you must deliver the presentation with conviction. In addition there are a number of public speaking guidelines which you should bear in mind:

- Use hand gestures and body language
- Establish eye contact
- Incorporate change of pace
- Use a variety of vocal pitches and volumes
- Keep good posture
- Do not jingle keys or change in your pockets

The qualities that you should project are warmth, honesty, openness, excitement, creativity, knowledge, confidence, and organization.

I recommend that you use notes, rather than text, to speak from. Prepare brief points that focus on the issues you want to address but still allow you to speak naturally. Your presentation should feel like a dialogue between you and the audience.

Never read your presentation from a text. You could use cue cards or, if you are using overheads or slides, have each visual remind you of what you wish to say. You will need to have a sufficient number of visuals to provide continuity to your presentation.

Encourage questions during the presentation rather than holding them until the end. This breaks up the presentation, giving it more variety and making it more interesting to the listeners. If the audience appears lethargic or passive, some planted queries from your team members may help awaken them.

Usually, more than one member of your project team will attend the interview. One person, probably the designated manager for the project, should take charge and act as the lead figure for your group. However, do not fall into the trap of having one person dominate the presentation and question period. The interview will have far more variety and interest if there is some back and forth between your team. You should plan in advance who should make which part of the presentation and who should field which questions. Rehearse some interjections and questions with your team.

Be client-oriented! Focus on how you will help the client solve problems and improve operations. Beware of speaking only from your point of view and only describing what you do and the terrific expertise you have. It is important not to challenge or threaten any existing beliefs. Instead, you need to build common ground.

Unique selling points should be included in your talk and should be very clearly stated in your introduction, the conclusion, and the body of your presentation.

The human mind can listen to a conversation using only about 15% of its power. To ensure that the other 85% does not drift off into other areas of interest, you must keep the listener's attention. The use of visuals is one good technique. My preference is for overhead transparencies rather than slides because you can keep the lights on in the room, allowing you to maintain eye contact and avoid sleepiness in the audience.

End the meeting on a high note.

If you place the transparencies yourself, you can move about the room, providing motion and variety. The figures you show should be relatively simple and uncluttered, done to a professional quality, and consistent in style. Your firm's logo should appear in the corner of each figure. The use of color will enhance the impact.

Your closure should sum up the key points or theme of your proposal and it should end on a high note. This is important as it helps awaken the audience (should you have allowed them to drift off) and, as it is the last thing they hear, it will have the greatest impact. Now is the time to summarize your USPs or list the key reasons that they should accept your proposal.

4. Taking part in discussion

The discussion after your presentation is probably the most important part of the interview. You must initiate a good dialogue with the client. This will probably start by the client asking a number of questions. Avoid the natural tendency after having given a presentation to continue speaking at length. Respond to these questions as briefly as possible while still giving a complete answer. There are several drawbacks to being too lengthy. In addition to annoying the client and potentially getting yourself into trouble, you will minimize the time to ask your own questions.

An important objective is to learn as much as possible about the client. For example, you should ask about operations, whether there are any problems (you may be able to provide assistance in areas other than the project under consideration), staffing levels, whether the client is currently using other consultants, pleasure or displeasure with current consultants, the background to this project, etc.

You also want to obtain some feedback on how the client feels about your proposal. Does he or she see some weaknesses? What are they? Can you reassure him or her that the concerns are unfounded or can be ameliorated?

Finally, you should not overstay your welcome. The client undoubtedly has a busy schedule and will appreciate your promptness. Once you have delivered your message and had some useful discussion, you should quietly depart.

5. Preparing the handouts

It is good practice to leave the client a handout to serve as a reminder of your firm and as a record of the meeting. I suggest you include a set of copies of the transparency figures you used and a personal cover letter and title page. You can enclose all the material in a folder bearing your firm's logo. Additional information, as appropriate, can also be included. Take the time to ensure that this package looks very professional.

> **There is enormous satisfaction in preparing a winning proposal.**

If appropriate, you could include with the handout a sample of your product, a pen or coffee mug with your firm's name embossed on it, or some other tangible object.

The hard copy "leave behind" has a number of purposes. It serves as a handy record of the meeting for the client and proposal evaluators. Furthermore, it allows you to again summarize your USPs. The handout also serves as a symbolic gift from your firm to the client and, as discussed earlier, builds a feeling of indebtedness that, it is to be hoped, will be repaid during the final selection process.

9

UNSOLICITED AND VERBAL PROPOSALS

The formal, competitive proposal described in the preceding chapters has one very significant feature: the client is in charge. He or she has requested that you prepare a bid package and you are responding to his or her invitation. Furthermore, the client wants to receive your bid and anxiously counts the minutes until the submission deadline.

But in the case of an unsolicited proposal, the potential client is not in charge, and that makes a world of difference. You may be seen as intruding, interfering, taking up valuable time, and so you must use your best persuasive skills to overcome this barrier. In most cases, you are trying to sell one of your brilliant ideas or concepts to someone, say your boss, your banker, or even your spouse, who has *not* solicited your idea. How do you go about it?

First of all, you must get the person's attention. This is not a trivial undertaking. Because your target is a human being, he or she will be consumed first and foremost with the problems and complexities of life. Remember Dave, the proposal evaluator from an earlier chapter — and remember the great distractions that he suffered under! Your recipient may have quite a different impression of your brilliant idea and may be annoyed that you are interrupting his or her busy schedule with some lame-brained scheme. Only after you have accomplished the first step of making your target receptive to listening, can you begin the task of persuasion.

Let's look at some situations in which you might wish to unleash your persuasive powers.

You must get your potential client's attention. This is not a trivial undertaking.

95

a. The "formal" unsolicited proposal

Another class of proposals is the formal unsolicited proposal. Quite often government departments have an unsolicited proposal program in which they do not issue specific RFPs, but do have some general guidelines and a budget set aside. It is up to the proposer to develop a project concept. This class of proposal is very similar to a solicited proposal in its structure and format.

University grants also fall into this category, in that there are guidelines and usually even an annual submission deadline. However, defining the scope of work is the responsibility of the proposer.

If you have a client you have dealt with for some time, and you have been taking the client-oriented approach, then you will undoubtedly be aware of areas where the client requires assistance. This is the perfect time and place to submit an unsolicited proposal.

Demonstrate the need for your product or service. Once you have accomplished this goal, it is easier to explain that your firm is the best one to deal with, since you are the only proponent of the idea. To convince them of the need you must understand the client's business.

Demonstrate the need for your product or service.

Develop a champion or mentor in the appropriate department of your client with whom you can discuss the proposal before you submit it. Lay some groundwork to establish whether there is a need for your idea. This contact will be a useful source of information, and an ally in the client's camp is particularly important for unsolicited proposals.

Example: An aspiring middle manager

Perhaps you are an aspiring middle manager and feel that you are ready for the responsibilities, and rewards, of a move upward. You have felt for some time that the company would benefit by expanding its operations into the western region. More important, the manager of this new division would be at a vice president level, and you would love to fill that role. Why not take the bull by the horns and make a proposal to management?

Prepare an unsolicited proposal that describes the scope of the division, has recommendations on how it should be staffed, includes a business plan with projected revenues and expenses, and so on. You should also list the pros and cons of the division and, of crucial significance, be able to clearly demonstrate that it is a viable concept. Some attention grabbers might include the growth of the company, the prestige of western offices, good profit, and diversification.

In this case you should prepare a memorandum proposal and send it to the appropriate senior manager suggesting that you meet to discuss it further.

Even in the remote possibility that your proposal is rejected, you will have gained considerable visibility in the firm and will have enhanced your chances of being selected for the next upward vacancy.

Example: The software entrepreneur and venture capital

In another scenario, you have spent the last ten months developing a software package that tracks the financial performance of companies and predicts their future trends. It is a useful tool for the unsophisticated investor who wishes to play the stock market on a part-time basis or as a hobby. All your friends who have tried it are enthusiastic, and their support has played a major role in your decision to try to bring the package into the marketplace.

In spite of the handsome stock market profits that you have reaped using the program, you still require additional financial support for your entrepreneurial idea. You decide to seek venture capital. But how do you proceed?

You need to prepare a business plan, which is just an impressive term for an unsolicited proposal. The business plan will need to be very persuasive, because no one, not even rich venture capitalists, will part with money without good reasons. Furthermore, venture capitalists are busy people. They are engrossed with managing their portfolios, reviewing other requests, and enjoying the fruits of their labors. In fact, finding new investments absorbs only a small part of a venture capitalist's day. Thus, you absolutely must have a good zinger, something to grab their attention.

Be brief and concise. In many ways, the appeal for venture capital is the ultimate test of your persuasive skills. The business plan will need to focus on profitability and the financial return to the investor. The four key factors are:

(a) The management team

(b) The service or product

(c) The market for this product/service

(d) How you plan to get the product to the market.

Develop projected cash flows. Include all the persuasive principles described earlier but don't make the recipient slog through unnecessary detail.

An executive summary is the most important part of the business plan because it may be the only part that gets read. It should pique the venture capitalist's imagination and inspire him or her to pursue your proposition.

Sell yourself as much as the product.

Next you have to find an appropriate venture capital firm. Not all such firms are created equal. Investigate them and find one that specializes in the kind of software that you have developed. If possible, interview some entrepreneurs that have dealt with these firms. Learn about the personalities involved and select a venture capital firm with whom you will be comfortable working.

Sell yourself as much as the product. Almost without exception, venture capitalists believe that the experience and track record of management is the most important component of a new venture, even more important than the product. Poor management can cause a good product to fail, whereas strong management can cause a mediocre product to succeed.

If possible, arrange an introduction to the venture capital firm that you have selected from a friend, accountant, lawyer, or mutual acquaintance. The business community is relatively small and introduction by a personal contact has far greater impact than a cold call or a package arriving in the mail.

As has been discussed, a face-to-face meeting is one of the most powerful methods of selling your ideas. This will allow you to demonstrate your software firsthand. Make sure that it will work without a hitch. A nice personal touch would be to demonstrate your program using firms in which the potential client has an interest. You may have to do some research in advance to have the necessary data already loaded into the software, but this shouldn't be too difficult as you have already researched the types of businesses this venture capitalist deals with.

The meeting will allow personal chemistry to work.

b. The main rules

As the examples above illustrate, the business world presents many opportunities to practice your persuasion skills. There will be many times when you have a chance to sell your favorite concept or your brilliant dream which may affect your promotion, your career, and even your personal happiness. But there are also minor skirmishes that go on all the time, day in and day out. You will certainly enjoy life more by recognizing and learning how to apply the persuasion principles to the different situations you encounter. Try to be more rigorous, analyze the situation, and apply the persuasion techniques in a methodical manner.

Here are a summary of guidelines, most of which were illustrated in the preceding examples, of how to deal with the ubiquitous unsolicited proposals.

1. Grab their attention

Grab your recipient's attention and do it quickly! You must overcome the initial mistrust of your intrusion into their time and space. Convince them that it is in their best interests to listen to your proposition. You cannot, for example, have a long and rambling cover letter. You must be short and snappy. You must pique their curiosity and this can only be done by knowing something about them. In other words, your attention grabber should be client-oriented.

2. Sell the need for your idea

The key is to sell the need for your idea. Why is it required? What will it do for the recipient? Be totally client-oriented and demonstrate how your proposal will enhance and improve his or her operations or life. The techniques discussed in chapter 4 are applicable here, but now they are subordinate to the client-centered approach.

Unique selling points are not as important for unsolicited proposals. Now, there are no competing proposals and your idea must sink or swim on its own merits.

Similarly, your own qualifications may take a subordinate role to the client-oriented approach. Nevertheless, you must establish your technical credentials and capability to successfully perform the undertaking.

3. Be brief

Be brief! You are intruding into a person's busy schedule so you must be as succinct as possible.

In contrast to the solicited proposal, I recommend you include an executive summary. Certainly, when seeking venture capital or a contract, the executive summary is absolutely critical. If it does not grab the attention of the reader, your proposal will be doomed to the giant garbage bin of rejected proposals.

4. Identify and neutralize negatives

You must identify and neutralize the perceived negatives associated with your proposal. This will require some analysis. There may be a good reason why what you are proposing has not been implemented earlier. For example, for the aspiring middle manager, perhaps the firm had been badly burned in a previous expansion into new territory. Do not try to sidestep such issues. You will need to meet negatives head on and demonstrate why your proposal is different and why it will succeed where others have failed.

5. Use all relevant persuasion principles

Of course, in an unsolicited proposal, all the persuasion principles (i.e., empathy, indebtedness, scarcity, etc.) that are used in solicited proposals also apply. You will need to tailor these to the specific situations that you face.

6. Build common ground

In particular, you should work to build common ground with the recipient of your proposal. In the example above of the aspiring middle manager, common ground was built with your senior management by showing that the western region fits into corporate objectives and style. In other words, a common vision was displayed.

7. Do not attack existing beliefs

Never attack the existing beliefs or status of the recipient of your persuasion. Ensure that your proposal is structured so it does not threaten any of the existing senior managers, particularly those who will be involved in the evaluation of the proposal. It does not pay to be negative about some other person who may also be a logical candidate for the position, particularly if he or she has as a mentor one of the influential senior managers.

10
THE LAST WORD

In today's hectic world, it has become commonplace to simplify even complex undertakings with a short, pithy list of instructions. So here, to summarize many of the concepts discussed in this book, is a list of DOs and DO NOTs for writing your proposal.

DO:

Make a sound decision — go or no-go

Develop USPs

Read the RFP very carefully

Study the principles of persuasion

Call the client if you have questions

Take the time to get the price right

Develop a standardized approach, with a library of templates

Go the extra mile

Keep it clear and simple (use lists, tables)

Nurture those that can write proposals

DO NOT:

Indulge in wishful thinking

Wait to the last minute to start

Use complex language and jargon

Send in sloppy work

Have a large proposal-writing team

We have reached the end of our journey. We have explored the complex workings of the proposal. We saw that preparing a winning proposal is not a simple matter. We inspected the components that constitute a proposal and we have seen how to combine them into an integrated and persuasive whole. This journey has shown the importance of presenting the proposal clearly and simply so that the proposal reviewer's task is made easier. We have also seen the importance of writing proposals quickly and efficiently and the impact this has on the bottom line. Above all, the proposal process is competitive — in order to win, the proposal must be very persuasive and have unique features which make it stick out from the crowd.

We have learned that there are basic psychological factors underlying persuasion and we have seen how these persuasion principles can be applied to creating a winning proposal. It is the skillful intertwining of knowledge and the psychology of persuasion that results in a successful proposal. We have also looked at how the persuasion principles can be applied to business meetings and other face-to-face encounters. Face-to-face meetings are an integral part of the proposal process.

You are now about to embark on the challenging voyage of preparing your own proposals. I hope you will find, as I have, that this voyage is full of excitement and fulfillment.

Although I have been writing proposals for over 15 years, the exhilaration has never diminished. My pulse quickens when a new RFP arrives. The process of preparing a proposal is like publishing a newspaper; the proposal preparation area, like a news room, is alive with energy. There is organized pandemonium in the battle to assemble the document before the looming and unforgiving deadline. Phones ring, keyboards clatter, and photocopiers hum as you assemble the manuscript and make final revisions in the hope of adding that critical persuasive ingredient. I find it exciting to be part of such a team, and I love the challenge of seeking innovative ways to make the proposal more persuasive than those of my competitors. I hope that you will share in this excitement.

Ultimately, I hope that writing proposals will bring you satisfaction. There is enormous fulfillment as well as enjoyment in the act of creation, whether it is a work of art, an engineering project such as designing a bridge or a dam, or a literary work such as a novel or a magazine article. Similarly, the creation of a proposal requires craftsmanship, hard work, and talent. The satisfaction is magnified when your creation wins.

I hope the underlying persuasion principles described in this book will be a valuable ally in your life. Interactions between human beings in society involve an ongoing series of proposals and your persuasion skills will be constantly used and tested. Society consists of unique individuals with their own goals and agendas, and conflicts between different people are inevitable. Without a certain amount of accommodation, society would become discordant and unorganized. Thus, persuasion (i.e., presenting proposals) is an important societal tool, not just in business, but anywhere you seek to resolve conflict. Persuasion has long been recognized as a prominent social skill.

In closing, I hope that this book in some small way will help you realize a greater excitement and satisfaction in the business world of proposals as well as in all aspects of your life.

Good luck and may all your proposals be winners.

BIBLIOGRAPHY

Burrill, G.S., and C.T. Norback. *The Arthur Young Guide to Raising Venture Capital.* Blue Ridge Summit, Pennsylvania: Tab Books, 1988.

Cialdini, R.B. *Influence — How and Why People Agree to Things.* New York: W. Morrow and Company, 1984.

Connor Jr., R.A. and J.P. Davidson. *Marketing Your Consulting and Professional Services.* New York: John Wiley and Sons, 1985.

Hamlin, S. *How to Talk So People Listen — The Real Key to Job Success.* New York: Harper and Row, 1988.

Hillman, H. *The Art of Writing Business Reports & Proposals.* New York: The Vanguard Press, 1981.

Holtz, H. *Writing Winning Proposals with Your PC.* Glenview, Illinois: Scott, Foresman and Company, 1990.

Meador, R. *Guidelines for Preparing Proposals.* Chelsea, Michigan: Lewis Publishers, 1985.

The New Encyclopaedia Britannica. Various articles on psychology, persuasion, and motivation. Chicago, London, Toronto: Encyclopaedia Britannica, 1981.

Vardaman, G.T. *Making Successful Presentations.* New York: Amacom, 1981.

OTHER TITLES IN THE SELF-COUNSEL SERIES

PREPARING A SUCCESSFUL BUSINESS PLAN

Rodger D. Touchie
$15.95

If you are considering a new business venture or rethinking an old one, you need to document your long-term plans. This book will help you create an effective proposal for achieving goals in the form of a business plan. Recognizing that a business plan constitutes much more than a written document, this guide will enable you to lay the foundation for a dynamic process of planning, reviewing, and updating your business agenda. By completing the worksheets, you will set the foundation of your internal planning process for years to come.

Includes:

- Basic elements of business planning
- Identifying your target audience
- Creating a mission statement
- Developing a marketing strategy
- Defining your team members
- Preparing a financial plan
- Presenting an impressive document
- Future planning procedures
- A sample business plan

MARKETING YOUR PRODUCT

Donald Cyr and Douglas Gray
$11.95 USA / $14.95 CDA

An informative planning guide that covers all the essentials, this newly updated and expanded edition demonstrates how to carve a niche for any product in today's competitive, fast-paced, and often fickle consumer environment. This long-trusted guide provides step-by-step advice using plenty of helpful worksheets.

Includes:

- A new chapter on the Internet
- Effective advertising venues
- Measuring consumer behaviour and pricing right
- Achieving maximum distribution
- Successfully establishing products in foreign countries
- How to develop a competitive edge

MARKETING YOUR SERVICE

Jean Withers and Carol Vipperman
$11.95 USA / $14.95 CDA

Service businesses today face stiff competition — nine out of ten new businesses are in the service sector. Accountants and lawyers, hairstylists and health club owners need to understand the distinctive nature of marketing a service, and each must devise a custom-made strategy to succeed. This book will help you plan and execute an effective marketing campaign.

Includes:

- Where to find information about potential clients

- What you should know about your competition

- How to develop and implement an action plan for marketing

- Promotional strategies for success

ORDER FORM

All prices are subject to change without notice. Books are available in book, department, and stationery stores. If you cannot buy the book through a store, please use this order form. (Please print.)

Name _____

Address _____

    Charge to: ❏ Visa   ❏ MasterCard

Account number_____

Expiry date _____

Signature _____

Shipping and handling charges will apply.
In Canada, 7% GST will be added.
In Washington, 7.8% sales tax will be added.

YES, please send me:

_____ Preparing a Successful Business Plan

_____ Marketing Your Product

_____ Marketing Your Service

❏Check here for a free catalogue

IN THE USA

Please send your order to:

Self-Counsel Press Inc.
1704 N. State Street
Bellingham, WA 98225

IN CANADA

Please send your order to the nearest location:

Self-Counsel Press
1481 Charlotte Road
North Vancouver, BC V7J 1H1

Self-Counsel Press
4 Bram Court
Brampton, ON L6W 3R6

Visit our Web site at:
www.self-counsel.com